Words of Life

The Bible Day by Day
January–April 2012

HODDER &
STOUGHTON

First published in Great Britain in 2011 by Hodder & Stoughton
An Hachette UK company

1

A CIP catalogue record for this title is available from the British Library

ISBN 978 1 444 70310 8

Typeset in Sabon and Scala Sans by Avon DataSet Ltd,
Bidford on Avon, Warwickshire

Printed and bound in Great Britain
by Clays Ltd, St Ives plc

Hodder & Stoughton policy is to use papers that are natural, renewable
and recyclable products and made from wood grown in sustainable forests.
The logging and manufacturing processes are expected to conform to the
environmental regulations of the country of origin.

Hodder & Stoughton Ltd
338 Euston Road
London NW1 3BH

www.hodderfaith.com

Contents

From the writer of *Words of Life*

First of all, I want so say it is a great honour and privilege to be the new writer for this devotional book. I sense already that God wants to bring both inspiration and encouragement through these writings, as we look into his Word each day. During the next three years we will be surveying each book of the Bible, as well as many topical subjects relevant for today's world. The overall theme for 2012 is 'Faith'. This edition looks at 'Faith in Action'.

We begin with the creation account and humankind's beginnings in Genesis. From there we move to the book of Exodus and see how Moses' faith brought the Hebrew people from bondage in Egypt across the Red Sea. After forty years of wandering, they finally arrive at Mount Sinai – receiving the Ten Commandments. Each commandment has its implication for twenty-first-century Christians, as we strive to live lives that are holy and pleasing to God. Moses then recounts the Hebrews' history in the opening chapters of Deuteronomy, in order to strengthen the people's faith.

In the New Testament we reflect upon the lives of the disciples, seeing how their faith was challenged into action as they responded individually to God's call upon their lives. When God calls us, how do we respond? Are we always willing to obey? Do we trust him completely with our lives? It's so important to learn from those who have gone before us.

Each Saturday we look at either one of the Psalms or a proverb. Although written hundreds of years ago, they still are applicable for today, helping us to put our lives into perspective and in alignment with God's will for each of us. On Sundays we look to a church hymn or a song out of The Salvation Army's songbook. These are rich in theology and inspirational in the way they speak to the heart.

Our guest writer for this edition – Captain Mal Davies, from Australia – looks at a variety of choruses used for both young and old. He then leads us helpfully into Passion Week.

God's Word encourages us to put *our* faith into action. He wants us to be used as his instruments in a world that is in such desperate need of Christ – the resurrected Lamb of God.

May God richly bless you as you meet daily with him in sweet communion.

Beverly Ivany
Toronto, Canada

Abbreviations

New Year Beauty

Let us continually offer to God a sacrifice of praise – the fruit of lips that confess his name (v. 15).

> For the beauty of the earth, For the beauty of the skies,
> For the love which from our birth, Over and around us lies,
> Father, unto thee we raise This our sacrifice of praise. (*SASB* 28)

Today marks the beginning of a brand new year. Our hearts want to sing for joy – not only at God's magnificent creation which surrounds us, but also in anticipation of all that's to come in this year for each one of us.

We want to bring 'our sacrifice of praise' to our Lord and Saviour, just for who he is. How can we praise him? We can certainly praise him in song – by singing from the depths of our being. We blend our voices with his, in adoration and thanksgiving for a new year; for health, family, and friends; for creation itself. As the hymn by F. S. Pierpoint states:

> For the mystic harmony Linking sense to sound and sight.
>
> (v. 3)

Giving praise to God can be done through the reading of Scripture, as we *continually offer to God a sacrifice of praise* (v. 15).

Praise can also be given through prayer. It is mysterious how God hears our praises and accepts them as our gift-offering to him. Enjoying his creation, enjoying his very presence pleases him.

Finally, we can praise him by loving him, and loving one another. It is interesting how the author of this song speaks of love in reference to gentleness of thought (v. 4): to be gentle in our approach to others; to embrace this wonderful fruit of the Spirit in our interactions – spoken or unspoken. Beauty in its truest sense.

Let us be a thankful people this year, living in a spirit of praise in all we say and do. May we daily give to God our sacrifice of praise.

> For each perfect gift of thine To our race so freely given,
> Graces human and divine, Flowers of earth and buds of Heaven,
> Father, unto thee we raise This our sacrifice of praise.
>
> (v. 5)

The Beginning

In the beginning God . . . (v. 1).

Beginnings are exciting! They are filled with such anticipation and expectation. Yet when we think of the beginning of time, the beginning of the world as we know it now, it's mind-boggling! It's mysterious, and beyond our human capacity to comprehend. The notion, the fact of God having always been, having always existed is virtually incomprehensible.

Creation of the world is fundamental to our faith. In fact it is the foundation of all Scripture, basic to its authority and authenticity. For God is supreme; above all, in all, through all. He also cares for you, for me, with a passion.

The beginning of a new life is beautiful; or the beginning of two lives joined in marriage. One could even say the beginning of a new job or new ministry appointment is energising. So is the beginning of a new year. With new beginnings comes the expectation and anticipation of something good and wonderful. What will today look like? Or tomorrow? What does God have in store for me?

In 1796 the masterful composer, Joseph Haydn, began work on his oratorio, *The Creation*. This was a profound act of faith on his part, being a deeply religious man. When he finished this particular work, two years after its commencement, he remarked that it was the most devout piece of work he had ever written. The act of creation was fundamental to his faith, thus he hoped his work would somehow change the way people thought of God in a positive and affirming way. *The Creation* was, indeed, a testimony to his faith.

Our faith tells us God is the source of creation. We are not here by chance. We are not just part of some unfeeling 'big bang' force. We are part of God's magnificent creation which is both intimate and extremely personal. It is, in fact, beyond our imagination.

In the beginning . . . God. The Creator of the universe chose you, and me, from the beginning of time. Let us, at the commencement of this new year, express our love and deep adoration to him.

Heaven and Earth

In the beginning God created the heavens and the earth (v. 1).

Creation is indeed a miracle. It is beyond our finite comprehension. C. S. Lewis says in his book *Miracles*:

> I do not maintain that God's creation of nature can be proved as rigorously as God's existence, but it seems to me overwhelmingly probable, so probable that no one who approached the question with an open mind would very seriously entertain any other hypothesis. In fact one seldom meets people who have grasped the existence of a supernatural God and yet deny that he is Creator.[1]

True, we cannot scientifically prove God's creative power. But by faith Christians believe he always was, and is, and will be. We also believe he is the Creator and still continues to create.

We are part of Earth, strategically placed in the colossal solar system. Our solar system is part of the vast Milky Way galaxy – containing, we are told, 300 to 400 billion stars. How many galaxies are there in the universe? Astronomers tell us there are roughly 100 to 200 billion of them, each with hundreds of billions of stars.

Humbling! Although it is hard to comprehend, even with our God-given intellectual capacity, faith encourages us to believe that our God and Creator, who flung all those stars into space, and who splashed both the heavens and Earth with its beautiful hues, loves us – more than we could ever imagine.

In God's creative plan, he made provision for us to have a relationship with him – fellowship. Also to have a deep connection to one another, and creation itself. God is the fount of life. The universe, the heavens and Earth, have purpose and meaning. This is why we are here – to worship God, to enjoy and care for Earth, and to share God's good news with others.

As we daily seek his sense of meaning for our lives, God will continue to illumine each of us. May we continue to fulfil this mission of reaching out to others, telling them of both his creative and redemptive power. What a God we serve! What a God we adore and love!

Light of the World

And God said, 'Let there be light . . .' (v. 3).

Light brings life. In Scripture we read that light was created even before the sun. Have you ever thought of this before? Creation is indeed mystical, and also magnificent. And it's all about God. In fact, creation verifies and affirms that everything originates with him, and is created by him – according to his perfect plan.

The Bible then says that, on the very first day of creation, God saw the light he formed, and it was good. It was a perfect reflection of his thought. Darkness was not good, for it was incomplete. So God separated darkness from light. To separate means to put into different places. Therefore, order in the universe was being carefully formed. There was definite purpose for the light.

Light became day; darkness became night. Everything was being set in motion. The rotation of day and night became a distinct pattern. Light, darkness; dawn, sunset; the first revolution of Earth on its axis. The first day was completed. And it was good.

The spiritual insight is evident, for God is all about light! Light is life. Light gives guidance. Light reveals wisdom. Light is revelation. Light is transformational. Light assures safety. Light radiates sheer beauty – for with light one sees the glorious foliage, the stunning skyline, the kaleidoscope of colours all around – created for our pure enjoyment. Light reveals all things, and illumines the soul.

Day, night – and so the natural, extraordinary, blessed rhythm of God's creation began. Light for the day, yes; but also the needed rest for the night. Rest – to restore and renew the body, the mind and also the spirit.

Evening, then morning – we are now refreshed, ready to carry out God's will for the day. We become energised, eager to fulfil the perfect design he has for each of us. A vital plan, entrusted to us; mandated to give us purpose, and give God glory and honour. For the world is in desperate need of God's redemptive light.

Prayer

Shine, Jesus, shine – so that we may reflect your light today!

Andrew – the Tenth Hour

'Come,' he replied, 'and you will see.' So they went and saw where he was staying, and spent that day with him. It was about the tenth hour. Andrew, Simon Peter's brother, was one of the two who heard what John had said and who had followed Jesus (vv. 39, 40).

He knew when it happened; the exact hour when he encountered Jesus. It was the moment Andrew turned from his past life to his future. The tenth hour launched a new and exciting life for him – that of fellowship with Christ, the Messiah. It was the hour of not only opportunity, but also one of eternal destiny.

From then on, there was no turning back. Andrew first brings his brother, Peter, to Jesus. Then he thinks of others he can also lead to Christ, so that their lives, like his, would be changed forever.

Several months pass, following that life-changing tenth hour. A crowd has gathered, listening to Jesus. It has been a long, hot afternoon. No one has eaten. There are no restaurants; no one had thought of bringing food – except one small boy.

Andrew notices him and sees that he has a lunch with him. He tells Jesus, and brings the boy to him. Not much in the little sack to eat; and again, a child? Quite insignificant, children; not even recorded statistically. Yet look what Jesus does with that little boy's small offering. And the boy himself . . . recorded in history forever! An event he would never forget, as long as he lived. It was a moment of amazing grace; a 'tenth hour' experience for him, no question.

When was it for you? Perhaps you cannot recall the exact hour or moment you turned from one life to another. Yet most of us can name a time or times when Christ became real in a powerful way. A moment when, similar to Andrew, we turned our lives around and followed; as an adult, or perhaps as a young child.

Andrew also wanted others to know Christ. He reached out to his brother. He approached a young boy, with a lunch. The Lord wants us to also reach out – having an 'Andrew heart' in desiring others to be transformed by Jesus into his likeness.

Yes; amazing grace . . . the *hour* I first believed!

Andrew – My Unbelievable Story

The first thing Andrew did was to find his brother Simon and tell him, 'We have found the Messiah' (that is, the Christ). And he brought him to Jesus (vv. 41, 42).

I led my brother to Jesus. Peter (Simon) became more prominent than me in many ways. He was the one who was the leader, being more upfront by nature. He was certainly noticed more by people. Yet I take certain pride in the fact that it was me who introduced him – an introduction that virtually changed Peter's life.

Maybe if it had been someone else, Peter wouldn't have paid any attention; wouldn't have followed through. But he trusted me. He believed that if I felt he should at least get to know who this Jesus was, it was definitely worth the investigation. And look at the outcome! Not only for Peter himself but also for the Church at large.

I knew Peter was gifted, and could offer so much. This is why I sought him out. My name soon became second to his. But I was perfectly content with this. After all, beautiful music can come from those who play the second part! Perhaps, at times, they might even have a fuller, richer sound – the harmony, the enhancement; the support, the complement.

Many are not in first place, and subsequently struggle with this. Yet the reality of life is, far more are in second or even third place. Not in charge. Not the boss. However, we can all still make a valuable, even vital contribution in whatever place we find ourselves. In the eyes of God no one is more important than another. Male, female, old, young. All are equal in his eyes. The key is being content with who we are, knowing we are all created in his image – reaching out to others in the name of Christ.

Jesus chose me, Andrew. He actually chose me first, in fact. Why? Because I believe he trusted me enough to bring others to him. Each one of us is to touch the lives of others, in order to turn the world upside down. What a difference we can all make, for Christ's sake. Will you be bold enough to tell others of Jesus' extraordinary love – today?

New Year Delight

Blessed is the man . . . [whose] delight is in the law of the LORD, and on his law he meditates day and night (vv. 1, 2).

To be blessed is indeed something wonderful! The Hebrew word used in the Bible here is in the plural. It tells us that, if we live our lives according to God's plan and design, God will indeed give us multiple blessings. This doesn't mean that we will be trouble-free, nor even rich by world standards. But we will be *blessed* – over and over again.

When we're blessed, there is suddenly a compulsion to soak it all in; to bathe in all God's Word has to say to us; to 'delight' in all it has for us, as we are nourished and fed daily. The desire is to be ever-present with the Creator – to meditate on who God is, day in and day out.

We delight in God, especially at the commencement of a new year; for we wish to begin afresh, with a revitalised energy. We want to be obedient to his Word. The psalmist clearly indicates that there is a right way of living and a wrong way. Black and white. There are really no grey areas – although some try to excuse certain actions by living in this blurred realm. It all comes down to choice. When we choose God's way, there is great delight in his heart. When we choose the wrong way, it grieves him deeply.

Blessings abound, when we are in tune with God, resulting in fruit; good things developing because of right choices made. It then further blossoms into lives filled with God's grace. What joy! What sheer delight!

We are all unique creations. If we stay close to our Creator, our path of life will eventually lead to the destiny God has planned for us. It's up to us how we want to live out this new year. Will it be according to his spectacular plan for us?

Prayer

Father, I long to delight in your abundant blessings today. Help me to meditate on you and your Word this year. Create in me a renewed thirst that is unquenchable. Hear my prayer, O Lord.

King of Creation

Praise the LORD, O my soul; all my inmost being, praise his holy name (Psalm 103:1).

Praise to the Lord, the Almighty, the King of Creation (*SASB* 19).

This great German hymn, '*Lobe den Herren*', written by Joachim Neander in the seventeenth century, gives praise to the Creator of the universe. Some might ask: 'Why does God deserve to be praised?' Let us think of a few reasons (suggested by the hymn itself).

- *Creation* How blessed we are to be part of God's vast creation! He could have stopped with the sun and moon, the stars and the waters, the trees and flowers, the birds, reptiles and animals. But no; he wanted to have intimate communion with each one of us.
- *Health and salvation* Some think it's wonderful to have wealth, or fame. But without health, there is not much we can do. And what about salvation? Christ, dying for us – so we can have eternal life in him. This truly is cause for adoration!

The hymn goes on to speak of his

- *Goodness and mercy* – day in and day out. They both follow us, as the psalmist reminds us, *all the days of our lives* (Psalm 23:6). Indeed, we should ponder anew the implications of what this all means for us.

There will be days when there is *warfare*; when the elements rage all around us. Days when we don't know where to turn, for everything will seem to be falling apart for us. It is in these times that the Lord comes, often when we least expect it. He bids the raging to cease, and turns it into an inner peace – like nothing else.

We are not perfect people. So far from it! Satan tempts. Sometimes we do fall. Yet the glorious news is, God forgives, and he also cleanses. And when he *chaseth the horrors of night* away, he brings us closer to himself.

Yes, our Lord and our God. How you *deserve* to be praised. How we want to lift our eyes to you, today, and sing to the King of creation!

Praise to the Lord! O let all that is in me adore him!
All that hath life and breath, Come now with praises before him! (v. 5)

Two Trees

And the LORD God made all kinds of trees grow out of the ground – trees that were pleasing to the eye and good for food. In the middle of the garden were the tree of life and the tree of the knowledge of good and evil (v. 9).

When things go wrong in our lives, because of poor decisions we make, we often slide into what psychiatrists call today 'psychological projectionism'. Basically it is projecting the blame for our actions on someone else – parents, siblings, spouse – for our behaviour patterns. It's not really new, is it? When caught, Eve blamed the serpent; Adam blamed Eve. And on it goes. We know the story well.

There were two trees in that beautiful garden. One was the tree of life, representing the goodness of God – life itself. In the following chapter in Genesis (v. 8) we read of God walking in the garden with the trees 'in the cool of the day'. What a beautiful, idyllic image! In the miracle of nature itself, God always appears. For he brings life and laughter; he brings peace and purpose for life. There is complete synergy when we speak of trees, a garden, God in the midst.

Yet also in that garden was the tree of the knowledge of good and evil. It was not a choice to be made between a good tree and an evil tree, for God does not make anything evil. If he had, or if God had programmed people to disobey him, it would be a concept like the Hindu idea that eventually both good and evil, cruelty and non-cruelty, spring from God and thus are finally equal. This is simply not true.

There is nothing intrinsic about this particular tree that is any different from other trees. Rather, God simply confronted Adam with a *choice*. To obey, or disobey.

All love – man to woman, woman to man, friend to friend – comes down to choice. Without choice, love is virtually meaningless. And so, the choice is ours to make. To obey or disobey God's directives. To love him, with all that we are, or to turn away from him.

Today, let us make the right choice – and love him completely!

Pandora's Box

Now the serpent was more crafty than any of the wild animals the LORD God had made (v. 1).

God created, and he saw that it was good. And it was *very* good when he created man, then woman – for now he was able to commune intimately with them, with his created people. Fellowship! But suddenly, something went terribly wrong.

Although we do not believe in myths, they often give us certain insight. There is a story in Greek mythology, for example, that encapsulates some of the main themes of the fall. A legend tells us that Zeus chose the Titan Prometheus to go to Earth – in order to create man. Prometheus was to give something to man, to make him supreme over all creation. He gave to man fire. But the other gods, collectively, thought man would then become equal to them. So a new plan was devised: the creation of woman – to be more captivating to the man than fire.

When she was created, Prometheus's brother, Epimetheus, took this first woman, Pandora, to be his wife. Pandora was told she could have and do anything; but *not* to open the box in their new home. But she did; and out flew a host of evil plagues: disease, envy, strife, spite, revenge, sin. She tried to put the lid back on, but it was too late. Now there would be no danger of man being a rival to the gods, for humankind had too much to contend with on Earth.

The fall. Disobedience. They had everything, Adam and Eve. But they wanted more. They wanted to be as powerful as God himself.

'You will not surely die,' the serpent said to the woman. 'For God knows that when you eat of it your eyes will be opened, and you will be like God, knowing good and evil' (v. 4).

Temptation's five-fold sequence is still in effect today: curiosity; exploration; anticipation; sin; disobedience toward God. This is the very reason why God desires and longs for intimate fellowship with us. Today, may we seek the *fire* of the Holy Spirit – to reject temptation, conquer sin, and to have victory in Christ.

Fourfold Alienation

The LORD God called to the man, 'Where are you?' He answered,
'I heard you in the garden, and I was afraid because I was naked; so I hid'
(vv. 9, 10).

Fear entered the world at the time of the fall. Adam was afraid of God. Before this, the world was at complete peace. Beauty, like nothing else. Wholesome, and pure. Intimate and sinless communion with God.

But when sin manifested itself, in all its ugliness and corruption, there was immediate alienation. First, people versus creation:

'Cursed is the ground . . . It will produce thorns and thistles' (vv. 17, 18).

Second, alienation of man against himself. Inner turmoil. Fear within. Adam became aware of his nakedness, and was ashamed. Yet, knowing this would happen, God provided animal skins for him to cover himself. A blood sacrifice one day would cover *everyone's* sins – the cross.

Third, because of sin, there is alienation between man and woman. God said to Eve:

'He will rule over you' (v. 16).

Finally, there was alienation created between people and God. The peaceful Garden of Eden was created for humankind – with the intention of living forever. But the Lord banished them from this eternal bliss. Death would now become a reality:

After he drove the man out, he placed on the east side of the Garden of Eden cherubim and a flaming sword flashing back and forth to guard the way to the tree of life (v. 24).

Because of the cross, however, eternal life *can* and *will* be ours – if we put our faith in Christ. Today, let us praise him for redemption – his forgiveness and salvation – and his provision of grace for all.

Philip – Practically Speaking

The next day Jesus decided to leave for Galilee. Finding Philip, he said to him, 'Follow me' (v. 43).

When gathering information on the disciple Philip, it doesn't take long to discover that he was a very practical man. He always wanted to keep things on track. Similar people today might be those who keep lists, agendas, are constantly checking off things accomplished, and who can't sleep properly until everything is set for the following day. Maybe you know someone like this – maybe it's yourself! Some are simply wired this way. Philip was like this.

Because accuracy was important, perhaps faith was a little difficult for Philip. At times it seems as if he was struggling with it all. For there was no real *proof* that Jesus was the Son of God. His heart was in it, no question: but perhaps there was just a bit of intellectual hesitation. Belief wasn't something he could simply put on a list, then check it off. Pragmatists, like Philip, need to see the evidence; they need to work it out, to have a strategy, to live out the plan. However, faith doesn't really work this way.

Philip was no doubt tentative at times. He gained ground slowly, being cautious and careful. He seemed to have common sense, being meticulous and not missing a beat. Jesus saw something very noble in him, and said: 'Follow me.'

Some of the disciples sought out Jesus. But not Philip. He was too practical; too unsure about all he had heard about Jesus. He wasn't easily swept off his feet by a travelling evangelist. So it was Jesus who took the initiative and sought out Philip – seeing great potential in him. Because of the way it came about, Philip in return saw something in Jesus that was real and authentic. He took the step of faith, dropped everything, to follow – changing him forever.

Thought

Are we willing to drop everything, even for an hour, just to *be* with Jesus – to bask in his presence?

Philip – My Amazing Story

'Nazareth! Can anything good come from there?' Nathanael asked. 'Come and see,' said Philip (v. 46).

I looked into his face, and I just knew. It's hard to explain, really. Someone says to you, 'Follow me', and you simply drop everything, to obey. You leave your life, as you once knew it, to follow. Nothing like this had ever happened to me before. It still overwhelms me with deep emotion when I think back to that moment in time. As soon as Jesus spoke to me that day, joy enveloped me. I ran to my friend, and shared what had happened:

'We have found the one Moses wrote about in the Law, and about whom the prophets also wrote – Jesus of Nazareth, the son of Joseph' (v. 45).

I had to be sure. I had to check the prophecy again – to know for certain that the Messiah was to come from Nazareth, the son of Joseph. It all had to make sense, and it did. It was real! My friend objected, even questioned all I was saying about something 'good' coming from Nazareth. I simply said to him in response:

'Come and see' (v. 46).

I knew where he was coming from, because I have always been somewhat sceptical myself. Yet, once I saw Jesus for myself I just knew him to be the one. I was so sure, so certain. My old ways kept creeping back, however. When Jesus was preaching to a very large crowd, he turned to me and asked about buying bread, because I was the 'practical one' I guess. I told him that even eight months' wages would not buy enough bread for each to have one bite (John 6:7). But Jesus already had a miracle in mind. My faith was still weak. Jesus was helping me grow – day by day. And I *did grow* in my trust, my faith, my belief. He, in fact, transformed me.

I pray that you too will respond to Jesus and receive the affirmation of God's love. To be completely changed by him. For me, nothing else will ever compare!

World Rage

Blessed are all who take refuge in him (v. 12).

From the beginning of time, it seems, there has been war and continual rebellion. Nation against nation; ruler against ruler – all striving for ultimate power, control, and supremacy. The result is violence, terrorism, chaos, extreme rage. People want to do what they feel is their right, no matter what the cost. To sin, to rebel against God; to crush, humiliate, conquer, defeat.

Worldwide turmoil is all around us. And people want to show their power by breaking *chains* that might hold them back; by throwing off *fetters* that may constrain or hinder them in some way. God looks at this, as Scripture tells us, and *laughs* (v. 4) at their threats of dominance and control. For he knows who oversees all things; he knows who truly is supreme and in control.

In this messianic psalm, God introduces his Son – the one who is the ultimate ruler over heaven and Earth. For he is the anointed one, the chosen one. Yet it grieves his heart to see what has happened to his creation – the world, and all who live in it.

There may not be war happening where we live at present. But there could be evidence of rage in our cities, in our communities. People wanting to control others; people desiring to dominate; people abusing; people manipulating. They are people angry with the world which surrounds them. Rage. Yet God warns them, telling them:

Serve the LORD with fear and rejoice with trembling. Kiss the Son, lest he be angry (vv. 11, 12).

Kissing the Son refers to humility, reverence, devotion. For when we treat others with respect, when we acknowledge God's supremacy, when we acknowledge our servanthood, only then will we be able to enjoy all God has for us, taking refuge in him.

May we be instruments of his everlasting peace. May we reflect, in our personhood, the likeness and beauty of Christ.

The Secret of His Presence

'Go out and stand . . . in the presence of the LORD' (v. 11).

> In the secret of thy presence, Where the pure in heart may dwell,
> Are the springs of sacred service And a power that none can tell.
> *(SASB 591)*

This beautiful meditative song, written by General Albert Orsborn in 1920, was composed very early one morning by candlelight – when the General felt a real sense of God's presence. Of course, we know that God is always near us. We see him in creation, or in the face of a child. We acknowledge his presence when we bow our heads to ask for a blessing over our food. At night, before falling asleep, we know that he has been with us throughout the day.

Yet there are certain times that are very precious to us – when God comes to us in an intimately profound way. It's just us and him. It's private; it's a closeness that is hard to describe. He's just there.

Genesis 28:16–22 tells us of one of these times. Jacob had gone through some rough experiences. He came to Bethel, and simply needed to sleep. He used a stone for a pillow. Then he had a spectacular dream about God and his majesty. When he woke, he exclaimed:

'Surely the LORD is in this place . . . How awesome!'

Later in time, Elijah was discouraged because the Israelites had turned their backs on God once again. The Lord instructed him to go to a mountain, a cave. Following a powerful wind, an earthquake, then fire, there came a gentle whisper:

When Elijah heard it, he pulled his cloak over his face and went out and stood at the mouth of the cave (1 Kings 19:13).

God's whisper – in the secret of his presence. From then on Elijah knew of God's power, and his constant abiding presence with him. May we too know, intimately, of this glorious secret presence.

> In the secret of thy presence, In the hiding of thy power,
> Let me love thee, let me serve thee, Every consecrated hour.
> *(refrain)*

My Brother's Keeper

Then the LORD said to Cain, '. . . If you do what is right, will you not be accepted? But if you do not do what is right, sin is crouching at your door; it desires to have you, but you must master it' (vv. 6, 7).

The outcome of the fall took effect immediately. Cain and Abel were the first children. But there was instant jealousy. God gave to Cain a choice, knowing this jealousy was deep in Cain's heart. Cain could have quite easily rectified his situation. He could have changed, bringing an offering that *was* pleasing to the Lord – like his brother Abel had done. But no; he saw God's pleasure in Abel's offering, and God's displeasure with his own offering.

God brought this to his attention right away. Cain was given every opportunity, and sometimes we miss this crucial point in the account. However, he couldn't *master* the temptation to sin. He couldn't take hold of his strong, innate human emotional state, and give it to God. He went to the opposite extreme, by seeking out his only brother and committing murder.

Most wouldn't ever contemplate such an outrageous action – although it has happened, as we all know. Yet most of us do experience at times jealousy, which can be so detrimental to our life of holiness. This explosive emotion can take over our entire being: our thought-life, our actions, our spirit – all being darkened and often distorted. Cain was said to be 'downcast' (v. 5) to the extreme.

After the tragedy, the murder, the Lord sought out Cain and asked him where Abel was. Cain's response:

'I don't know . . . Am I my brother's keeper?' (v. 9).

This violent account from the beginning of time is written for us to learn; to see the repercussions of sin. A reminder, right from the beginning, to seek God's face when tempted. Also, to realise we *are* each other's keeper. Only when we realise this will our offerings be acceptable to the Lord – our offerings of love, joy, thanksgiving, praise. Today, tell the Lord you love him – with all your heart!

The Ark

The LORD was grieved that he had made man on the earth, and his heart was filled with pain (v. 6).

We have heard it so many times. Noah. The ark. A children's story. We can skip over this one. But should we? There are even obvious discrepancies. In chapter 6, the animals enter two by two. In the following chapter, it's seven by seven – coming from different historical documents. And so, the varying accounts blend together, even causing some to question the story's validity as actual fact. After all, there are flood stories in most major religions.

Probably the best approach is to read the story as historical, also as a parable. Historical in the fact that it's recorded in God's Word. A parable in that it illumines a life situation which helps us see God's ultimate purpose and direction for his children.

People's hearts were against God in Noah's day. There was no need for God. And today? Many do not even think of God. There is wickedness, corruption, violence. Read any newspaper. Life is cheap, it seems. Ambition, greed and envy rule. Abuse is rampant, taking many forms. And God grieves.

There was chaos on the earth; and God wept over his creation. His judgment upon the people became operative. It became a horror movie – no children's story. For sin is very serious business. Yet God found Noah, and his family. A family who sincerely tried to resist temptation. People who trusted God fully, and looked to God for strength and guidance in the confusion of life itself.

The ark was made as a protection. Noah was saved because he was righteous, and 'walked with God' (v. 9). Yet sin is still with us: war, evil, hatred, mockery of God through deliberate disobedience. God searches for those who walk with him; to shield them with his protective *ark* against Satan's attacks.

Prayer

Lord, protect me today. Help me to look only to you for guidance and direction for my life. Help me to trust you, completely.

Rainbow

'I have set my rainbow in the clouds, and it will be the sign of the covenant between me and the earth' (v. 13).

Explorers have recently claimed to have found the remains of Noah's ark, located four kilometres up the side of Turkey's Mount Ararat. They have uncovered wooden beams and compartments they claim housed the animals. Carbon-dating has proven the structure to be roughly 4,800 years old.

No matter what we or others think about this discovery, the account of Noah does not end with the ark. It ends with the rainbow, the promise, the covenant. God told Noah he would never abandon his creation like this again. It was a new beginning.

Creation is our responsibility; to care for it, and to protect it. But this story goes beyond caring for the physical world around us. It is about our love for and devotion to God. Then to reach out – caring for the *inner* world. People's hurts; people's brokenness. To share with others God's redemptive plan.

When the rains stopped, Noah finally emerged from the ark and made a sacrifice to God. Then God told Noah they could now eat meat. Also, that he was providing for them a whole new way of life. The ancient Israelites from then on wanted to thank God for his many provisions; and so, every time they ate together, it became an act of worship. It became a sacrament. To feed on God – enabling our spirit to unite with his. A oneness.

This amazing story culminates with the rainbow, the covenant. Yes, the protection of creation. But of even more importance, the bond made between God and humankind:

'Whenever I bring clouds over the earth and the rainbow appears in the clouds, I will remember my covenant between me and you and all living creatures of every kind' (vv. 14, 15).

Today may we reach out, perhaps even out of our comfort zone, to tell others of Christ's love, forgiveness and hope for the world.

Thaddaeus – the Unknown Disciple

These are the names of the twelve apostles: first, Simon (who is called Peter) and his brother Andrew; James . . . and his brother John; Philip and Bartholomew; Thomas and Matthew . . . James . . . and Thaddaeus; Simon . . . and Judas Iscariot, who betrayed him (vv. 2–4).

There is virtually nothing said about Thaddaeus in Scripture. Yet he was one of the chosen apostles. One of the twelve. He was called by Jesus, and was obedient to that calling.

The three years he spent with Christ were like nothing else in his life, we assume. He was asked by the Son of God to follow him, and he did. He walked with Jesus, shared life with him. They were three years of intimate, daily communion with Christ himself. Thaddaeus probably never took a single moment for granted, treasuring every word spoken, observing every act of extreme kindness shown. He would have noticed Jesus' touch – reaching out to children, the sick, the elderly, the marginalised.

Some might wonder why Jesus chose someone like Thaddaeus, since no special qualities or giftings are noted. We know nothing of his background, his family, or his occupation. Why him? Perhaps he was chosen because he had the right spirit of obedience, and surrender. Perhaps he was chosen because of his capacity to love.

Thaddaeus would have seen and witnessed the torture then crucifixion of the one who became so dear to him: Christ – the perfect person, who lived for others and not himself. He would have also witnessed Jesus' glorious, miraculous resurrection. He must have gasped in utter amazement, realising he witnessed everything with his own eyes. He no doubt was humbled by it all; that he had been chosen to be part of history in this wonderful way.

Following Jesus' ascension, Thaddaeus would have been spreading the good news of Christ to all who would hear, even if his own life was threatened. For he knew it was absolute truth.

God calls all of us unto himself. Then he urges us to spread the good news to others. Are we up to the challenge, even today?

Thaddaeus – My Transformational Story

'A new command I give you: Love one another. As I have loved you, so you must love one another. By this all men will know that you are my disciples, if you love one another' (vv. 34, 35).

I want to share with you something wonderful, as an apostle and disciple of Christ. For it's something I believe you would want to hear, and experience for yourself. It's true; I was changed, completely, when Jesus called me by name to follow him. We spent three glorious years roaming the countryside, listening to the Master preach; seeing people healed – physically, emotionally, spiritually. It's hard to put into words, the time spent with him.

Toward the end of our time together, he called us all to share a final meal with him. He told us he was soon to die; that it would be the end of this part of the journey as we knew it. At the meal he disclosed a betrayal to come. How could anyone experience the passionate love of Jesus, then betray him? Yet we are all human: afraid, vulnerable, egocentric. We mess up – often big-time.

He also said one of us would deny even knowing him. It could have been any of us, I guess. When it came down to it, would we really give up our lives for him? I'd like to have been able to say yes. But I'm a weak, selfish human being. Pitiful, I know.

Yet this is not all I want to share with you. I want to tell you what he said to us in that holy and sacred time, between referring to Judas and Peter. He told us simply to *love one another*. I say simply because it seemed so obvious, such a given; although, as macho men, we didn't often verbally say 'I love you' to each other.

So, why did Jesus stress this? Why was it so vital that he should tell us, just before his scourging and ultimate death, to love one another? I think what he was trying to convey, with the intention that we should share it with generations to come, was that we are to incarnate Christ; to be 'marked' by his love. To emulate his love; who he was, and is.

Dear friends, I pray this may be lived out in each life; loving one another – always. Then people will truly see the living Christ!

A Father's Heart

To the LORD I cry aloud, and he answers me from his holy hill (v. 4).

David wrote this particular psalm after fleeing from his son, Absalom. Can we even begin to imagine the anguish and inner turmoil he was experiencing emotionally, and even spiritually? Can we imagine going through this ourselves – actually trying to escape the death threats of our son or daughter, out of sheer envy and hatred? David loved him so much, for he had a father's heart. Sadly, the love was not reciprocated, and all because of greed and the insatiable desire for power.

Yet, although experiencing such deep pain in his personal family life, the heartbreak of his son turning on him in such a blatant and public way, David turned from his personal sorrow and grief to the Lord for strength and comfort and assurance. For God was his protector, his *shield*; he was always there for him, to bring encouragement and strength in times of great, personal need:

But you are a shield around me, O LORD (v. 3).

What are we facing today? Sometimes people, even close family members, let us down. Some even turn on us, for some reason, which breaks our heart. We cry out, as did David:

Arise, O LORD! Deliver me, O my God! (v. 7).

Only God can bring healing and comfort to a broken heart.

There are no doubt people near us, also, who may be deeply hurting; people with mother or father hearts – deeply wounded because of various circumstances. They may be fragile, yet in desperate need of God's love and restoration.

May we reach beyond ourselves, in order to bring a sweet balm of healing to another. May his blessing of deliverance be a soothing oil, poured over someone in need today.

Peace in Our Time

He will proclaim peace to the nations (v. 10).

Peace in our time, O Lord, To all the peoples – peace! (*SASB* 827)

As we commence this new year, we all pray it will be a year of peace in our world. We look around us; we read the newspapers; we listen to the news. Unrest and instability are everywhere, it seems. Now, perhaps more than ever before, we need peace among the nations. But it has to begin with ourselves.

Verse 2 of John Oxenham's hymn commences with the following:

Too long mistrust and fear . . .

Sadly, for many, there is a lack of trust in their own personal lives because of circumstances that have taken place. They no doubt live in certain fear – physical, emotional, even spiritual – because of the long-lasting effects. This can translate into negative outcomes, which can then be projected upon others. There is no inner peace.

The following verse, however, goes on to say that we need to lay everything aside, and turn completely to God. In our personal lives, yes; but also as it relates to the world in which we live. Only then can there be any kind of reconciliation and resolve.

O shall we never learn The truth all time has taught . . . (v. 3)

Yes, sometimes we are slow learners! We do want peace – for the world, for ourselves. Yet we never seem to learn from our past. We need to hold on to the assurance that God is the 'architect' for our lives; to inspire, in order that we be a people of peace.

It is then, as the final verse reminds us, that we will be able to 'build a glad new world' together, that is indeed peaceful. For one day Christ will return, and as the prophet Zechariah proclaimed hundreds of years ago:

He will proclaim peace to the nations. His rule will extend from sea to sea and from the River to the ends of the earth (v. 10).

Noah – Skeleton in the Closet

'Blessed be the LORD, the God of Shem!' (v. 26).

When we think of Noah, we automatically go to the ark, and the rainbow accounts; his wonderful family being saved. This story is told to children, and we relay to them the importance of loving God; also, of being faithful and obedient to him, no matter what is asked of us.

But soon after the family came out of the ark, and had the assurance of the covenant God made with Noah and creation, something happened – which was not good. It was a family skeleton. It had to do with alcohol, and more. This righteous man of God, this preacher and leader of the day, got drunk – and was completely hung over, naked. He fell asleep in his tent, having gone against God's will.

Whether it is too much alcohol, or something else that is not of God, the pattern is the same. When we sin, when we mess up, we fall – and usually fall miserably, for there is disgrace and shame.

Ham went into the tent; and Scripture tells us he *saw* Noah, his father. Some scholars go into detail about what the word 'saw' could mean, in this context. Suffice it to say there are tragic implications here. Noah had sinned, and there were serious consequences for that sin. Noah, when he awakes, speaks – and sad to say, these are the only words we have in Scripture from Noah's lips. He curses, not Ham, but Ham's son – his grandson, Canaan. From then on, Canaan and all his descendants would become the lowest of servants, eventually being conquered by the Israelites.

At the end of this tragic situation, Noah redeems himself by blessing not Shem, but the God of Shem. He wants to give glory to God for what God would do through Shem's descendants. We know these descendants to eventually be Abraham and the Hebrew nation.

It's all about God's grace, God's forgiveness. Good things can come from tragic situations. Today, let's make certain we are right with the Lord, cleansed and forgiven. Then the day will be filled with his divine presence and his awesome glory as we walk with him.

Lord of the Nations

From these the nations spread out over the earth after the flood (v. 32).

Noah's family multiplied and were scattered over all the earth. Genesis 10 speaks of his three sons and their descendants – not particularly inspirational reading for most of us. Yet they are not merely names of people; rather, the movements of people and nations throughout the ancient world.

Japheth, Noah's firstborn, is mentioned first, with his descendants. He was the ancestor of what we often refer to as the Gentile nations; the distant nations, the outer limits of civilisation at that time. Ham's descendants, on the other hand, settled mostly in what later became known as Canaan, as well as Egypt, Palestine and Saudi Arabia.

Shem, the middle son, with all his descendants, migrated to the eastern hill country. From Shem we move into the story of Babel, as well as the genealogy of Abraham – and eventually the story of the Hebrew nation as a whole.

Why, one might ask, is this chapter – containing lists of name after name – of any significance to us today? Because it gives us our roots. Jehovah God is the Lord of the nations; the God of both geography and history. He controls all, for he created all. Yet, for certain nations he had a specific plan and purpose. God chose the nation of Israel; then, he used other nations to achieve his direct purpose, in reference to the Hebrew people as a whole.

Noah's three sons left a mixed legacy to the world. Yet the Lord of the nations was over everything, for it is ultimately God's story. He cares for all the world. And he longs for all nations, all people, to know him and accept him as Lord and Saviour.

Prayer

Lord God of the nations, we pray for our world. We pray that people, in some way, will come to know of your love. Help us to share something of you with someone who today is in need of your love and grace.

Tower of Babel

'Come, let us build ourselves a city, with a tower that reaches to the heavens, so that we may make a name for ourselves and not be scattered over the face of the whole earth' (v. 4).

God gave to Noah and his sons a command to be fruitful, to increase in number and to fill the earth (9:1). What was their ultimate response? It is in today's Scripture verse. People wanted to make a name for themselves – probably the first declaration of what we have come to call humanism today. Self-advancement.

God knew what they were up to; he knew of their selfish ambitions and intentions. Thus, he responded and, interesting to note, it is a Trinitarian response, for he uses the word *us*:

'Come, let us go down and confuse their language so they will not understand each other' (v. 7).

When this actually happened, they stopped building the tower; then the Lord scattered them. The world became a different place, for the linguistic differences were a new phenomenon. They became confused, not knowing where to turn. Their world was turned upside down – as a result of their defiance against God.

St Augustine once spoke of the Tower of Babel in his book, *City of God*:

But what could the empty presumption of man have achieved . . . whatever the height to which that building towered into the sky in its challenge to God . . . [for] the safe and genuine highway to heaven is constructed by humility, which lifts up its heart to the Lord.[2]

According to Wycliffe Bible Translators,[3] there are now 6,909 languages throughout the world. Of those, only 438 have a complete Bible translation. More than 2,200 language groups don't have a single verse of Scripture available in their language. This is the tragedy of Babel – because of pride and self-exaltation. Augustine had it right: only those with a humble heart, those with the right motive deep down, will see God. May we *see* him today.

Nathanael – the Mystic

When Jesus saw Nathanael approaching, he said of him, 'Here is a true Israelite, in whom there is nothing false' (v. 47).

Sometimes the lists of disciples' names are confusing. For example, in the Gospels of Matthew, Mark and Luke the name Nathanael does not appear; rather, the name Bartholomew does, linking him with Philip. In John's Gospel, it is Nathanael's name that is linked with Philip. We presume it's the same person – Nathanael Bartholomew; Nathanael, son of Tolmai.

Nathanael is a man without hypocrisy, a man who is real. What you see is what you get. He is not looking for wrong motives, nor is he deceitful. Yet he seems to be somewhat of a mystic, the aesthetic one, sometimes even absent-minded. He's always thinking godly things. One who dreams. An introvert, and not particularly interested in details. Yet one who loves deeply.

Although practical people move things along and get things done, they always want to be on schedule, and sometimes get burnt out. Mystics, on the other hand, seem to be in another zone, another world at times. People can get frustrated with them, wondering if they are getting anything 'accomplished'; wondering if they are pulling their weight. But just as we need the extroverts and the practical people in life, so do we need the contemplative people, those who give certain insight that others may miss.

Jesus sees Nathanael from a spiritual perspective. He knows that Nathanael sees things at face value. He is true, honest and transparent. He is not afraid to share who he is with others. And it's interesting to note that he is a friend of Philip, the practical one. Philip encounters Jesus, then goes to his friend, Nathanael.

We *all* need each other; for we are all different and unique individuals with varying personalities. Yet we are one in Christ. God calls us all. Let us celebrate and value our diversity today.

Prayer

Father, make us one. Help us to accept and love each other.

Nathanael – My Incredible Story

'How do you know me?' Nathanael asked. Jesus answered, 'I saw you while you were still under the fig-tree before Philip called you' (v. 48).

I said something terrible once – something I'll never forget. And you won't forget it either, as it is recorded in Scripture forever. When my good friend, Philip, first told me about Jesus, I responded with, 'Can any good thing come from Nazareth?' (see v. 46). How I wish I could take back those biting, sarcastic words! Not because you now read this about me, and my quick tongue, but because of what happened after – and how my life was completely transformed. For Philip simply responded with: *'Come and see.'*

When I did go and see, prejudice suddenly vanished; sarcasm was blurred away. For Jesus, when he first saw me, basically said there was nothing false or subtle about me! I quickly asked this man from Nazareth, Jesus, how he knew me. He then said he knew me while I was still under the fig tree – even before Philip introduced me to him. I then knew, for certain, that this was the promised Messiah:

'Rabbi, you are the Son of God; you are the King of Israel' (v. 49).

He knew me! Can you believe it? I needed no other proof. Some may say I was too quick to believe. But everyone comes to Jesus in different ways. I had been praying for the coming Messiah for years. Then, when it actually happened, I was transported in my spirit to another world. For I knew him to be the Son of God.

Jesus was aware that I was a bit of a mystic; one who was always reading, and praying, and contemplating the things of God. And because of this, he said to me:

'I tell you the truth, you shall see heaven open, and the angels of God ascending and descending on the Son of Man' (v. 51).

I *did* see all these things! He has things for all of us to see, daily. Be in his presence, and so, enjoy him fully today. Contemplate him; meditate upon him. Just take time for him. I know you'll never regret it!

A Fool's Paradise

The fear of the LORD is the beginning of knowledge, but fools despise wisdom and discipline (v. 7).

We live in a world that is populated by many seemingly foolish people; people who settle for a life of mediocrity. Some might dare say meaningless lives; empty. They go about their day-to-day routine, not caring; with no real interest in anything of worth. No discipline, carrying an apathetic attitude in all they do and say.

Some of these same people go to the extreme – contemplating suicide. And we know that this is on the increase in many societies, especially among younger people. But most do not go to this extent. Rather, they just laze about. They often speak out, and protest about society at large – utterances made without really thinking things through. But who really cares? Nothing seems to matter.

Even in church, the word *sin* is not often mentioned. One might 'slip up' in some area; but most things can be explained away by situational ethics. After all, people don't want to offend others, or turn them off. They don't want 'heavies' laid on them. It's hard enough, some think, just to stay afloat. Day to day. That's all.

Fools. We don't speak of them, really – even though the Bible mentions quite a bit about them. We might read about fools in a Shakespeare play: 'Life is . . . a tale Told by an idiot, full of sound and fury, Signifying nothing.'[4] Nothing seems right, or makes sense. For there wasn't much to these fools – emotionally or intellectually.

Foolishness. Sure, all of us do foolish things. People laugh. Sometimes, there are those who 'act the fool'. Yet, there is so much more! God wants our lives to count for something. Not for our sakes necessarily, but for his. To be a disciplined people. Rather than living in a fool's paradise, to have the insatiable desire to get only the very best out of the life he has given to us.

Rather than becoming trapped in a fool's bleak utterance of despair and futility, let us be wise, and shout in a firm acclamation: 'I am yours, Lord, and you are mine.' *This*, indeed, is true paradise!

My Father's World

'See . . . new things I declare' (v. 9).

> This is my Father's world, And to my listening ears
> All nature sings and round me rings the music of the spheres. (*SASB* 42)

The American Maltbie D. Babcock wrote the above words in the late nineteenth century. He would often say, as he left home each morning, 'I am going out to see my Father's world.' He then wrote a poem around this thought, which is now a hymn. What do we *see* each morning, as we leave our home? Do we intentionally acknowledge our Father's world each day?

- *The sounds* Do we listen for the song of the birds? If yes, what are they singing about? Who are they singing to? Their Creator? Perhaps we hear the squealing sounds of children playing, or dogs barking. If near water, the lapping of waves against the shore. If in the city, the traffic whizzing by, the horns, the chatter of people in the streets. Let us be attentive to the various 'music of the spheres'.

- *The sights* What will we see today? Perhaps the 'rocks and trees', or the 'skies and seas'. There is such beauty, everywhere! It's there, every day, all for our enjoyment. Yet sometimes we get so caught up in the busyness of life, failing to notice our Father's world. The psalmist reminds us to always be attentive to God's creation:

> *When I consider your heavens, the work of your fingers, the moon and the stars, which you have set in place . . . all flocks and herds, and the beasts of the field, the birds of the air, and the fish of the sea . . . how majestic! (Psalm 8:3, 7–9).*

- *The smells* What beautiful aromas will we take in today? The smell of flowers; clean, fresh air; trees; grass; fresh snow; someone baking bread or pies; a roast in the oven. It's all ours for the taking.

Finally, let us remember: God rules over all. Even when there is discord and strife in God's world, one day all will be well!

> This is my Father's world; The battle is not done;
> Jesus who died shall be satisfied, And earth and Heaven be one. (v. 3)

Ur of the Chaldeans

Terah became the father of Abram, Nahor and Haran. And Haran became the father of Lot. While his father Terah was still alive, Haran died in Ur of the Chaldeans, in the land of his birth (vv. 27, 28).

Up to this point in time, it is very difficult to assign specific dates to what has taken place historically. But when we come to the account above, we can now approximate the date as around 2000 BC. From secular history, we know a fair bit about Ur. Thus, there exists a correlation between biblical and secular history – noting that this does not, in any way, imply that what came before this recorded account is not historical.

Sir Charles Leonard Woolley, both in 1922 and 1934, excavated the entire area of Ur. When we think of Abram, we often associate him and those around him with tents; the nomadic kind of life. However, the people at the time of Abram were far advanced in civilisation and culture. According to Woolley, they worshipped the moon goddess, and we are told that their houses were made of brick – even whitewashed for aesthetic purposes. These houses were often two storeys high, with up to ten to twenty rooms. They had kitchens that were well equipped, and had good plumbing systems.

And so, when God told Abram to pack up his things and leave this highly cultured area, to move to an area he would eventually show him, it must have taken much faith, sacrifice and courage:

'Leave your country, your people and your father's household and go to the land I will show you' (Genesis 12:1).

The key point here is that Abram, at seventy years of age, did not question God – at all. He may have wondered himself; he may have personally struggled internally; he may have grieved over the loss of his homeland; he may have wondered what lay before him. But he trusted God, with all his heart.

Do we implicitly trust God with today and tomorrow – no matter what he asks of us? For he'll be with us, every step of the way!

Extended Blessing

The LORD had said to Abram, '. . . I will make you into a great nation and I will bless you . . . and you will be a blessing. I will bless those who bless you' (vv. 1–3).

When Abram was obedient to God's voice, God gave him a threefold blessing. He was told he would personally be blessed; he would be a blessing to others; and finally, those who blessed Abram would also be blessed.

Isn't it wonderful to know we are personally blessed by God? Each morning when I pray, I always thank God for his bountiful blessings showered upon me. My family; my wonderful husband of many years; my four loving, adult children and their spouses; my tiny, precious little grandchildren; my godly mom, and the wonderful memory of my dad; my beautiful sister; good, faithful friends; my church family and place of work. I am truly blessed, beyond measure.

It is also amazing to know, through God's spirit, we can be a blessing to others. Sometimes I might question: Me? A blessing to another? Yet God uses me, I know. I pray each morning that he will 'make me a blessing to someone today'. And so I might call someone, write them a letter, pay them a visit, give a word of encouragement, do something practical to help another. To be a blessing is something beautiful, and it is something very good indeed.

Finally, it truly warms the heart to know that God blesses those who bless us. The extended blessing. I'm not sure what you're like but, for me, it's much easier to give than to receive. Yet receiving is a blessing, from someone who deeply cares about me. It's humbling, sometimes, for me to actually receive – for it makes me vulnerable. But it's a beautiful thing, to be blessed by another, then to know that, somehow, they will be blessed by God. Wonderful!

We serve an awesome God. Let us bless him today. Let us be thankful for his blessings. Let us be a blessing to another. Let us be open to being blessed. What a day is in store for us!

La Forza del Destino

She named him Moses, saying, 'I drew him out of the water' (v. 10b).

Four hundred years have passed since the close of Genesis. The good news: the descendants of the patriarchal family have grown into a nation of several million. The bad news: they have become oppressed slaves in Egypt. Yet we see in the book of Exodus God's redemptive plan in their release from bondage and God's establishment of a covenant relationship with his people.

It begins with the birth of a tiny baby. At the time of this birth, the Pharaoh of the day has no memory of Joseph nor of the Israelites' human rights. He has in fact come to despise the Hebrew people; thus he sends out a decree to kill all newborn Hebrew males. A certain Levite woman gives birth to her son during this dreadful time in history. She desperately tries to hide him, finally placing him in a little basket among some reeds along the bank of the Nile.

Pharaoh's daughter goes to this same river to bathe, sees the basket, hears the little cries of the baby, and falls in love with him. She's then approached by a young girl, offering to have the baby nursed by a Hebrew woman. The baby's mother will even get paid for nursing her own child! Eventually, the baby's mother passes him over. His new, adoptive mother names him Moses.

In 1862, people witnessed the first performance of the opera *La Forza del Destino (The Force of Destiny)*, by the Italian composer, Giuseppe Verdi. The premise of the opera is based on *circumstance* – the eventual destiny of the various characters, determined by where they are, at certain times and places. God-ordained destiny goes much further. Here we see the hand of God on everything that transpired, enabling Moses to grow and be the leader God eventually needed for the redemption of his people.

Each one of us is in God's hands. Not predestined, having no choice. But rather, people with a divine destiny in God's plan for our lives. May we always be in alignment with his divine plan for us – for today, and all the tomorrows to follow.

Matthew – the Money Man

'But so that you may know that the Son of Man has authority on earth to forgive sins . . .' Then he said to the paralytic, 'Get up, take your mat and go home' (v. 6).

He was a clever man, a Jew by birth. Matthew's goal in life was to make money, and plenty of it – no matter what others thought of him. He chose a rather unpopular occupation. Being a tax-collector was almost equated with being a prostitute in the days of the Roman occupation; for one was hired by Rome, the governing power, collecting funds to propagate Roman authority. Therefore, tax-collectors were shunned by fellow Jews.

Matthew became a publican to do this task. He didn't seem to mind that he was making money from his own people, for he was tough-skinned, and seemed to be able to live with himself. Who cared what others thought? It was his life, and his livelihood.

Then one day, something happened to Matthew. He noticed a man called Jesus. Everyone was talking about him. He heard what Jesus said to people, the way he was with others. On one occasion, people brought to Jesus a paralytic, lying on a mat. Jesus told the man that his sins were forgiven. Immediately, teachers of the law reacted. But Jesus knew their thoughts. He responded by telling the man on the mat to get up and go home.

A physical healing, yes. But far more significant was the assurance of a spiritual healing. It got Matthew thinking, deeply. What was he doing with his own life? What was his purpose, the significance of his existence? This man Jesus . . . could he be the promised Messiah? Could his life really change?

When Matthew was called by Jesus, he turned his life completely over to him – then used his mind, his skills, to write an account for us to read. In it, he never mentions his name, other than a reference to his calling. Humility took the place of greed. A changed man, inside and out.

Today may we look inward, then upward. May we learn from this man – to be a people desiring to change and submit completely, for Christ's sake.

Matthew – My Life-Changing Story

'If a man owns a hundred sheep, and one of them wanders away, will he not leave the ninety-nine on the hills and go to look for the one that wandered off? . . . In the same way your Father in heaven is not willing that any of these little ones [children] should be lost' (vv. 12, 14).

I was at my tax-collector's booth, my usual spot. People came by, paid their taxes, then left. No one ever stopped to chat. They treated me like the scum of the earth, actually. But I had gotten used to it. We all have to make a living. I took their jibes and their scorn in my stride. It didn't really bother me, most of the time.

Then one day something happened. I was minding my own business, tallying up the money that had come in that day from the people, *my* people, for Rome. Someone was standing at the booth. I could see him out of the corner of my eye, and sensed an unusual presence. When I looked up, I was immediately drawn to his eyes; eyes that seemed to be looking into the very depth of my soul. Two words – that's all he said. Words which spoke through my rather shady accounting, my ambiguous lifestyle, my empty life.

All of a sudden I felt dirty, empty. I felt like a thief; one who made money off my fellow Jews. Perhaps I hadn't heard correctly. For those two words he uttered that day were: 'Follow me.' When it sunk in, I found myself shutting my books, standing, walking away from that booth – never to return again. For I simply followed him, this man called Jesus. I felt, as I walked, somewhat in a daze, that everything was being stripped away from me: my pride, my selfishness, my ambitions, my arrogance, my guilt, my shame. And I didn't feel dirty any longer. I was clean, forgiven, at peace. I was a new man!

No longer Matthew, the tax-collector, the publican. Instead, Matthew, the apostle of Christ! There were no doubt hundreds, thousands of people he could have called. But for some obscure reason he chose the one who had gone so far astray, for his service.

He has chosen you also. And so, live a life worthy of that calling today. Like me, it will be a life-changing experience!

Shine Upon Us

Let the light of your face shine upon us, O LORD (v. 6).

The introduction to this psalm, in the *NIV* translation, states that it is 'For the director of music. With stringed instruments'. As we read through the eight verses contained in the psalm, let us do so imagining the soft musical background of the calming strings. It is peaceful. It is meditative; for the psalmist, David, beckons to the Lord to listen, and to answer his prayers.

The soothing music continues, as the soul cries out to God. There is certain distress present; for we often question the things life throws at us. We try to do what's right as we go about our daily lives – with family, with work, with various personal issues. But we're human; and sometimes we're thrown off track. Someone says something; someone does something. Or perhaps it's a circumstance that has taken place which is hard to get our head around. It disturbs us; it might even get us upset, and angry.

We must stop and listen to the music. God's music. To do as the psalmist suggests:

Search your hearts and be silent (v. 4).

Then we have the word *Selah*. This word, used twice in the psalm, indicates a pause. Stop. Listen to the beautiful sound of the instruments. Listen to God himself. When things get worked up within us, this is the time for deep reflection, and silence.

As the music plays, we can take time to bask in the light of God's face, which shines upon us. We can move through the day, seeking his strength and direction and guidance. When the day comes to a close, when the music fades away, it is then that we can thank God for who he is, and for what he means to us. It's then that we can unite our voice with the psalmist and say:

I will lie down and sleep in peace (v. 8).

His Love Has No Limits

He gives strength to the weary and increases the power of the weak (v. 29).

> He giveth more grace as our burdens grow greater,
> He sendeth more strength as our labours increase,
> To added afflictions he addeth his mercy,
> To multiplied trials he multiplies peace.
>
> *(SASB 579)*

This song is taken from *Annie Johnson Flint's Best-Loved Poems* (1957). It originally had the title, 'He Giveth More', with three scriptural references: 'He giveth more grace' (James 4:6); 'He increaseth strength' (Isaiah 40:29); and 'Mercy unto you, and peace, and love, be multiplied' (Jude 2).

Annie lost both parents before she was six years old. The Flints, desperately wanting a child, adopted her; but soon her health weakened. In her late teens, she was unable to walk, due to severe arthritis. What a childhood she had! What afflictions for a teenager! She pressed on. Music became a passion; she dreamt of becoming a concert pianist. But the arthritis took hold of her fingers, and she was unable to play. She then took to writing poetry, yet soon was unable to type. She persevered – typing with her knuckles.

How did she keep going? Annie knew, with all her heart, that God daily gave her more grace, more strength; his mercy increased as her afflictions became more prominent. As difficult as life was for her, both physically and emotionally, God multiplied his peace for her, his precious child.

What are we facing today? Prayer changes things. For, when we think we can take no more, when at the end of our rope, we are reminded of God's unlimited love and grace. The final verse affirms this truth for us – giving both assurance and confidence:

> His love has no limits, his grace has no measure,
> His power no boundary known unto men;
> For out of his infinite riches in Jesus
> He giveth, and giveth, and giveth again.
>
> *(v. 3)*

Holy Ground

'Do not come any closer,' God said. 'Take off your sandals, for the place where you are standing is holy ground' (v. 5).

M oses was far from being a saint. We are told he killed a man, forfeiting all the advantages he had hoped to use, to bring relief from the oppression for his people. Having fled to Midian he ended up, at the age of forty, sitting by a well, miserable. He had blown it; for he had taken things into his own hands, committing a terrible crime. Yet God delights in building cathedrals out of rubble. Moses' life was to be reconstructed, eventually to become a monument to God's grace.

Forty more years passed. Reconstruction takes time. Moses was now tending and caring for the sheep of his father-in-law. One day, an angel appeared to him in flames of fire from within a bush. From that bush, God spoke. And when he did, he told Moses to remove his sandals, for where he was standing was holy ground.

It is interesting to note the progression. In his twenties and thirties, living in Pharaoh's court, Moses must have thought he was a real *somebody*. But it all came crashing down on him when he turned forty. Then, having to flee and be isolated for forty more years, that somebody became virtually a *nobody*. He had to pay for the consequence of his sin.

But also, it was a time when God's refinement was taking place in his life, perhaps even without Moses' awareness. At the age of eighty, he was ready to be used in a mighty way. God can do something with those who are completely humbled. When we are stripped bare, finally realising we are nothing, we are then ready to respond: *'Here am I' (v. 4).*

Thought

Right now might be a good time for us to take off our shoes, wherever we are, and realise we are on 'holy ground' as we come before God. Let us reaffirm to God, once again: 'Here am I – ready to be used as your faithful servant.'

Leadership Development

But Moses said, 'O LORD, please send someone else to do it' (v. 13).

Moses had a wonderful 'burning bush' experience. He was to be God's person for a critical time in the history of the Hebrew people. Yet he lacked confidence as a leader. Forty years earlier, in Pharaoh's court, he seemed to be ready to take on the world. But God needed him to be humbled, refined, open to his leading.

His early training, at his mother's knee, was both crucial and essential. There cannot be enough emphasis placed upon the influence of parents in these formative years. Playing with children, spending time with them. Life-long impressions are made in these years – years to be treasured and so greatly valued.

Then, Moses lived in Pharaoh's court. Scripture tells us: *'Moses was educated in all the wisdom of the Egyptians and was powerful in speech and action' (Acts 7:22).* He could speak and perform well. Yet Moses took matters into his own hands one day, causing him to run for his life. He needed to be changed – from the inside out.

As we know, it took forty years in the desert for this to happen. Yet when God called him from that bush, Moses greatly lacked confidence: *'Who am I, that I should go?' (3:11).* Then further, what was he to say to his own people? Who was calling Moses? God responds:

'I AM WHO I AM' (v. 14).

In other words, the one true God – Jehovah, whose name was too holy to even be uttered – was, and would always be, with them. Moses needs further signs from God that he is to be the chosen one. And so, the staff turns into a snake, followed by his hand turning leprous. Yet Moses still pleads for God to send someone else.

God doesn't expect us to have it all together. In fact, if we think we have it all, then we are not ready to be used effectively for him. All God wants from us is our availability, our willingness. All he wants is our heart, open and receptive to his wonderful love.

We Shall Overcome

'I will take you as my own people, and I will be your God. Then you will know that I am the LORD your God, who brought you out from under the yoke of the Egyptians' (v. 7).

The Israelites did not have it easy. Life was very difficult for them – physically, emotionally, even spiritually. They not only blamed the Egyptians for their condition, but also turned on their newly appointed leader. Moses himself didn't know what to do, so turned to God, saying: *'you have not rescued your people at all'* (5:23). Pretty bold! But it showed the openness and honesty Moses had with his God.

The plagues were to come, God told him, which would eventually cause Pharaoh to let the Israelites go. But more than this, God would be giving his people the reassurance that he was with them, always. He had been with Abraham, Isaac and Jacob; he would continue to be with his people now. He considered them to be his *own*. There would be deliverance and rescue. In fact, there would be a promised land for them. Canaan would be theirs.

We are never promised an easy life. Some seemingly have it easier than others. Yet we don't know what is going on in another's life. Often there is great inner turmoil, deep struggles within. Sometimes physical hardship is even less painful than emotional pain. Spiritual depravity is by far the most difficult of all.

In 1901 the gospel hymnwriter Charles Albert Tindley wrote a song which included phrases like 'I'll overcome some day' and 'Deep in my heart'. Eventually, he added other lyrics to finally come up with the spiritual: 'We Shall Overcome'. The song has since been adapted and used worldwide – speaking of hardship and difficult times. Yet, as the song suggests, no matter what the circumstance, we can overcome – with God at our side.

Whatever we are facing in life right now, or anything that might come upon us in days that lie ahead, we are to know for certain that we can somehow get through it all. How? Because of God's strength, and his everlasting presence.

Simon – the Zealot

'I did not come to bring peace, but a sword' (v. 34).

When we read the list of disciples, we note that Simon comes in eleventh – just before Judas Iscariot. He is given the name of Zealot. And, other than these two things, there is nothing really said of him in Scripture.

The other Simon was also called Peter, listed first. The big fisherman; the spokesman for the whole group. But number eleven? Not much prominence there. Rather obscure, in fact. And what about those Zealots? They were a political party; fanatic patriots; a group of Jews believing in national freedom for Israel. There was to be no compromise with Rome.

The Zealots came into existence about twenty years before the ministry of Jesus. Many thought they caused the overthrow of Jerusalem in 70 AD – Rome versus Jerusalem, nearly forty years after the death and resurrection of Christ.

Simon was a freedom-fighter; a rebel; an extreme patriot, zealous for Israel. He wanted national, political and religious independence for his nation. With this kind of zeal and focus, why would Jesus choose him to be one of the twelve? Surely he would cause more trouble, than to be of any use to him.

But Jesus saw something in Simon. He saw him as being an integral part of his diverse group. Different personalities; different interests and giftedness. People who could collectively reach a world with a myriad of personalities and temperaments.

Also, he chose Simon *because* of his zeal and passion. He had determination – that could be channelled to do so much good for the kingdom. Jesus called him, then began to redirect his passion, his energy. Simon soon saw that the sword Jesus spoke of was a sword to destroy darkness and despair, only to bring peace and serenity. And so, Simon soon came to depend upon the sword of truth; to see not just freedom for Israel as a nation, but rather freedom for the whole world – all because of the cross of Christ.

Today, may we show zeal in all we do. May we demonstrate passion in all we say. And may our lives be lived for Christ, alone.

Simon – My Remarkable Story

He called his twelve disciples to him and gave them authority to drive out evil spirits and to heal every disease and sickness. These are the names of the twelve apostles . . . Simon the Zealot (vv. 1, 2, 4).

I was a Zealot – and proud of it. After all, what right did the Romans have, to come and rule us? To take over our identity and enforce their rules upon us? To make us pay taxes to them, and give us virtually nothing in return?

I was born with this fire in my bones. It was certainly a cause worth fighting for. It made me feel like I had purpose, direction. After all, I was fighting not only for my country, my nationality, but also for my religion.

We had no real leader as such. But then this man Jesus came and overturned the money-changers' tables; and he spoke of the 'sword'. Perhaps he was the Messiah – who would reign, and conquer! The one who would take over, and establish the throne of Israel. The one who would bring freedom from Rome. Jesus, leader of the Zealots! Yes; I was definitely interested in him.

But something happened which threw my life completely upside down. Rather than me choosing him, he chose me! I just couldn't figure it out. My new friend, Matthew, worked for Rome, collecting taxes. I, on the other hand, wanted to overthrow the Roman government! He was a tax-collector; I was a tax-hater. Two complete opposites – but both chosen by Jesus. Why?

In brief, all I can tell you for certain is that everything changed for me. I became refocused, redirected, recreated! The kingdom of God suddenly became everything to me. To the point of eventually giving my life, as a martyr, for Christ's sake.

No matter what kind of personality or gift-mix God has given to you, give it all over to him – for his use, for his service. Rededicate yourself to him, once again. Then reignite your passion for him, in a way you have never done before. I promise that you'll never regret it. Your life will be remarkable, just like mine, because of Christ!

Prayer for the Morning

In the morning, O LORD, you hear my voice; in the morning I lay my requests before you and wait in expectation (v. 3).

A morning prayer, offered to the Lord, speaks of a heart which desires the day to be dedicated to his service. It is not merely a habit; but rather an offering; a desired communion with God, in anticipation for what the day may hold.

C. S. Lewis, author of *The Screwtape Letters*, writes of Screwtape, a demon, and his instructions to his nephew, Wormwood, a novice demon. The premise of these letters is how to defeat and bring down Christians. As it relates to people praying, Screwtape advises Wormwood to 'interfere at any price' for 'real prayer is lethal to our cause'.

As the psalmist suggests, we are encouraged to lay our requests before God each morning. We are to praise him for who he is; to thank him for the many blessings he gives us. Then, we are to confess any sins, any thoughts that are not of God, in order to be forgiven and cleansed by him. Also, we are to intercede on the behalf of others; to put the needs of others before ourselves:

Spread your protection over them, that those who love your name may rejoice in you (v. 11).

Starting the day in prayer gives us fortification, encouragement, hope. It gives us a lift for the day. It gives to us the assurance that the Lord will be with us; that he will be a *shield (v. 12)* for us throughout the day. We can go forward in his strength.

Prayer is crucial. It is vital. Prayer puts us into a different sphere, a different space – soul space. It is a spiritual discipline that is to be embraced, and cherished; for it is an exercise that is essential for daily living. Let us pray . . . !

Trust and Obey

May your unfailing love come to me, O LORD . . . for I trust in your word (vv. 41, 42).

> When we walk with the Lord in the light of his word,
> What a glory he sheds on our way;
> While we do his good will, he abides with us still,
> And with all who will trust and obey.
>
> (*SASB* 397)

When we begin to take life for granted, it is then we need to do a reality check on our prayer life. For life happens. Things start to go wrong around us. All our plans, all we have mapped out in our minds, start to fall apart. What then? This is a crucial time when some might fall away, do something crazy, or even lose out completely. Yet it can be a time when we are pulled back into reality – into God's domain. A time when we reach out to him, in complete humility. A time when we trust him implicitly with our lives, willing to be obedient to his will.

The purpose of prayer is to speak, and also listen. Then, as the mystics often say, to learn that God alone is enough. When shadows or clouds come into our lives, as the song by John Henry Sammis reminds us, we are to trust – for 'his smile quickly drives [the doubts] away'. We are to trust him, and his precious word, completely.

Obedience should naturally follow. Fully trusting, as this song reminds us, is giving all to him. Until we do this, we cannot experience 'the delights of his love, until all on the altar we lay' (v. 4). The psalmist also says:

I will keep your law and obey it with all my heart (Psalm 119:34).

When we trust, and are obedient to God's will, what happiness is ours! Nothing can bring us such inner peace and abundant joy:

> Trust and obey, for there's no other way
> To be happy in Jesus, but to trust and obey.
>
> (refrain)

People of Character

And Moses answered, 'Look at me. I stutter. Why would Pharaoh listen to me'? (v. 30, MSG).

Moses may have had a speech impediment. And if this is true, he no doubt had an inferiority complex. He wanted someone else to be the leader, to be God's spokesman. He lacked confidence, believing no one would listen to him, especially someone as powerful as Pharaoh. He wanted to be of use; but he really felt he was inadequate for the task God had planned for him.

God was looking for a leader – yes, with skills; but far more than this, he was looking for someone of *character*. One who has character has far more than mere proficiency, or even intellectual capability or experience. Important as these things are, one's character is far more crucial. For these are the people God can depend upon; people who can reach out, and influence others. Character is who we see, the real person. Character is the transparent self. And when one's character has godly qualities, then God can use that person for his glory. He has plans, and promises to be fulfilled, for people with a godly character.

We may have a certain *title* in life. But it's our actions and behaviour which actually earn people's respect and cooperation. This is character. If we think we're the best, we can be easily beaten. However, if we always try to *do* our best, then we become winners in God's eyes every day. This is character. What you are is what makes you rich, not what you have. This is godly character. God-ordained happiness is not, in the end, our position in life, but rather our *disposition*.

Just as God promised to be with Moses and his stuttering speech, he promises to be with us – no matter what inadequacies we may possess. Above all, he is looking to our character, to who we are. People who are holy and pure in thought and intention.

Prayer

Today, may I be a person who demonstrates godly character.

A Hardened Heart

Moses and Aaron performed all these wonders before Pharaoh, but the LORD hardened Pharaoh's heart, and he would not let the Israelites go out of his country (v. 10).

The nine plagues found in chapters 7 through 10 were a devastating judgment of God upon the nation of Egypt. The Egyptians worshipped, for example, the mighty Nile River, believing it to be the bloodstream of the god Osiris. The water suddenly becoming undrinkable, with it actually becoming a form of foreign blood, was devastating. Frogs were associated with the goddess Heqt, and were symbols of fertility. But now they swarmed the land, causing distress and chaos. The gnats, or lice, rose from the ground – the land the Egyptians worshipped.

The flies (or, some scholars say, beetles) covered the crops, houses, even human bodies. The boils covered their bodies; the hail destroyed all their grain. All their livestock was destroyed. The total darkness was thought to have been an intense sandstorm, with some translations saying it was a thick darkness – an affront, in any way of looking at it, to their sun god, Ra.

With all that was happening, nothing affected the Israelites, who were living close by in Goshen. Then, the last plague was pronounced: the death of all firstborns – the animals, but of far greater significance, the firstborn of every Egyptian family. Yet still Pharaoh's heart was hardened. He could not admit that there was someone more powerful than himself. He was full of pride, full of his own self-interests, full of what the world had to offer him: recognition, prestige, status, fame, prominence, authority.

At times our own hearts can become hardened. God wants us to do something new, something perhaps out of our comfort zone. Yet we strongly resist; we say *no* to the deep spiritual prompting of the Spirit. Today, let us finally give in. Let us soften our hearts, in order to align with God's heart. Let us be free in him. For when we let go, it is then that we fly – like never before!

The Passover

'This is a day you are to commemorate; for the generations to come you shall celebrate it as a festival to the LORD – a lasting ordinance' (v. 14).

The plagues never affected the Israelites. God was protecting his people. And so, when the last plague was declared, God wanted full protection for his chosen nation. They were instructed to kill a lamb, then put the blood on the sides and tops of their doorframes. After this, they were to eat the meat with bitter herbs that same night, along with bread made without yeast. The yeast represented corruption; the bitter herbs, repentance.

They were to repent of their sins, and live holy lives, pure lives. And finally, there were specific directions on how to eat this Passover meal. It was to become a ritual for the Israelite people to observe for generations to come – a festival to the Lord. For they were soon to be delivered from bondage and oppression. This ceremony points to a greater redemptive work – that of the Messiah. Centuries later, John the Baptist declared:

'Behold, the Lamb of God!' (John 1:29, KJV).

The Lamb's blood was a covering, a protection from judgment – in this far greater way, as pointed out in 1 Corinthians:

Christ, our Passover lamb, has been sacrificed (5:7).

The slaying of firstborns came. Pharaoh finally, through the deep sorrow of losing his son, let the people go – at least temporarily. God's people were delivered, his people set free. The desire of God's heart today is still to bring people deliverance. May we be conduits for this total freedom in Christ.

Prayer

In remembrance of the Passover, Lord Jesus, I give my life to you afresh. Thank you for delivering me from sin, to everlasting life in you. May I dwell in your presence, and bask in your love.

Preparation for Lent

For forty days and nights he fasted, and at the end of them he was famished (v. 2, NEB).

Next week is the commencement of Lent. Although it is not particularly emphasised in The Salvation Army, many Salvationists observe it. If nothing else, we should be aware of its significance. For it can be a time of real spiritual growth, leading into Easter.

In the early centuries, Christians fasted for the two days before Easter. But by AD 325, at the Council of Nicea, the forty-day fast was established. Lent begins on what is known as Ash Wednesday and ends on the Saturday before Easter. Sundays are excluded – thus the forty days, relating to the forty days Jesus spent in the desert before beginning his public ministry.

In the early years Lent had a twofold function. First, it was a time set aside for repentance and self-denial. Second, it was to be a time for instruction in doctrine and creed – even for membership. During the Reformation, some wanted to eliminate Lent since the word is not mentioned in Scripture. Luther, however, wanted to keep it, for he saw this period of time as faith-building. Also, it helped Christians to focus, for a set period of time, on the Passion – the suffering and death of Christ. However, he felt Lent should never be mandatory, but strictly voluntary.

Lent is a spiritual discipline that should never be forced upon anyone. It can be a time set aside to really focus on Jesus and all he did, and is doing, for us. A time of spiritual renewal. Giving up something we enjoy can be a reminder of Christ's sacrifice. This can cause us to think of the cross, his sacrifice, in a deeper and more significant way – perhaps drawing us into a more intimate relationship with Jesus as we allow him to speak to us.

Prayer

Lord, as we approach this Lenten season, show me what you would have me do. Above all else, I want to draw into fellowship with you, and commune with you like never before.

Lent Anticipated

'The Spirit of the Lord is on me, because he has anointed me to preach good news to the poor. He has sent me to proclaim freedom for the prisoners and recovery of sight for the blind, to release the oppressed, to proclaim the year of the Lord's favour' (vv. 18, 19).

Are you thinking about Lent? Should you participate in it? Perhaps you are still giving this careful thought. Or perhaps you naturally look forward to this every year. Like all things, it should never become routine, or a ritual, but something to be anticipated. Some say it's not for them, and this is perfectly fine. It should never be forced upon people. But perhaps there are a few things you might want to consider, to actively live out this Lenten period.

First, you might want to give up something you enjoy. It might be coffee, or tea, or soft drinks. It could be candy or sweets. You might decide to fast for a certain number of meals each week. But it doesn't have to be only food. You might decide to fast from TV, or from computer games. It's to be a time of self-denial. It's giving up something, in hopes of relating to the supreme sacrifice of Christ.

Another way of approaching Lent is to *do* something for others. Perhaps making lunches for homeless people; visiting the elderly; contacting people to encourage them; organising weekly prayer times during this forty-day period. It's a time to think outside the box; to think of what you can do to draw closer to others, then ultimately closer to Christ.

Above all, it should be a time to meditate upon the Word. We should make sure we set aside time, daily, to read and pray; time to dwell on God's love for us; time to repent of our sins; time to ask for forgiveness; time to think of others before self; time to figure out how we can make a difference; time to realise where we would be without Christ at the centre of our lives. May it be a precious and coveted time, for us all.

Prayer

O Lord, help me to realise the importance of your Passion. And as we come to this Lenten period, may I commit to loving you more and more each day.

Wisdom Beckons

Wisdom calls aloud in the street, she raises her voice in the public squares; at the head of the noisy streets she cries out, in the gateways of the city she makes her speech (vv. 20, 21).

The World Wide Web, often referred to as 'www' or simply the 'web', is a global information medium which was developed in the 1980s. It's a service that operates over the Internet, as email does, containing intricate intellectual history. Most of us cannot comprehend how it works. Yet we are glad of it, and use it – for it has become part of our world.

Nearly 3,000 years ago King Solomon, perhaps one of the wisest people who ever lived, warned people about the neglect and ultimate rejection of wisdom in daily life. In other words, do we use each moment of every day wisely? Are we wise in our decision-making? Do we value and listen to the wisdom of others – no matter what stage we find ourselves in life?

Things are usually created to benefit us; to make life easier. When it comes to something like the Web, there is nothing intrinsically wrong with it – nor with the Internet itself. But wisdom is needed, as to how it is to be used. There are some things that are not good about certain websites, certain aspects of the Web. Some things could be detrimental to our spiritual well-being. On some websites, people are exploited. People can be sold. If not careful, our eyes could be spiritually damaged; our hearts, separated from God.

Solomon makes reference to wisdom calling out in the streets of our cities. She, wisdom, needs to be heard; for wisdom is essential for spiritual well-being and purity, vital for holy living. She also cries out in the public squares, the noisy streets, in the gateways of the city. City life can be exciting; it can also be dangerous.

Today, let us make wise decisions, asking the Lord to impart his wisdom to us – in all our transactions, in all we say and do. Whether they are public things, or private things, we need to be wise and true before God. To live a life that is only, and all, for him.

I Know Thee Who Thou Art

He will wipe every tear from their eyes. There will be no more death or mourning or crying or pain (v. 4).

> I know thee who thou art, and what thy healing name;
> For when my fainting heart the burden nigh o'ercame,
> I saw thy footprints on my road
> Where lately passed the Son of God.
>
> *(SASB 59)*

Most of us have been touched by sorrow. The death of someone close to us causes such great pain. Often, we don't know where to turn, or how to access any kind of relief from the deep agony we are experiencing. General Albert Orsborn went through such an experience with the death of his wife. This song of his was born out of severe grief in 1942. Penning these words helped bring certain relief and, in fact, gave to him a heart full of praise for his Lord and Saviour.

In the second and third verses he refers to God being with him on the road of life, bringing great delight in the 'sweet communion' they share; walking and talking together. He writes of the beauty in God's face, sustaining him through life's trials and difficulties.

Then in the final verse, which he records as his favourite, his soul soars forth in anticipation of being in heaven one day – eternal life with God. It will be a place with no suffering, no pain, no sorrow.

Even though we may be experiencing a very difficult time, or know someone in such pain, we have Someone always with us; Someone who loves us, more than we could ever imagine. Let us then hold nothing back from him. For, because of Calvary, one day we will be with him – forever!

> Let nothing draw me back or turn my heart from thee,
> But by the Calvary track bring me at last to see
> The courts of God, that city fair,
> And find my name is written there.
>
> *(v. 4)*

The Exodus

'On that day tell your son, "I do this because of what the LORD did for me when I came out of Egypt." This observance will be for you like a sign on your hand and a reminder on your forehead' (13:8, 9).

The command came from Pharaoh. Go! Leave Egypt. Words that the Israelites had been waiting to hear after 430 years of slavery. And with this new freedom, they were even given severance pay for all their accumulated forced labour: gold, jewellery, clothing. The Egyptians had been traumatised after all that had happened to them in recent days; thus, they were more than happy to give over their possessions, just to get rid of these people.

Roughly two to three million people left Egypt, along with all their livestock. God had told Abram centuries before that his people would leave the land of bondage with great possessions (Genesis 15:14). They left enriched by Egyptian goods; but they were also enriched because they were learning to depend upon God alone.

They travelled from Ramses to Succoth; but before long, God stopped everything – wanting to speak to them of remembrance and of family. He wanted the Israelites to be in constant remembrance of God's redemptive plan for his people, and to also remind them of passing this on to future generations.

A young mother went to hear a live performance by Paul McCartney, one of the former Beatles. She held up a poster, asking him to sign her back. He was intrigued, called her up on stage, and obliged with the marker she provided. The next day, she went to a tattoo artist and made the signature permanent.

People today get so caught up with people of fame, status; the powerful and the popular – even to the point of wanting this kind of lasting remembrance. God instructed his people to remember, and instil strong, godly, lasting family values into their children. Let us never forget to have the marks of God engraved on our hearts, forever. Signs, reminders that he is ours, and we are his.

Thought

All you (we) need is (his) love! May we embrace this, and live it!

The Sea

Then Moses stretched out his hand over the sea, and all that night the LORD drove the sea back with a strong east wind and turned it into dry land (v. 21).

The Israelites came to a seemingly inescapable dead end. It was at the intersection of Baal Zephon and the Red Sea when suddenly they heard the sounds of chariots in the distance. Pharaoh had changed his heart. How foolish he had been to let his slave labour escape. Now, he was coming to bring them all back. The Israelites panicked. The sea was before them. They were trapped. Doomed.

People often stand at a threshold, at the shore of a sea, crying into the night out of emptiness and despair. The world before them seems so dreadful, so empty. Life for many seems to be a tragedy. There seems to be no tomorrow in sight, nor any desire to go on. Perhaps some of us have been there ourselves. Or at least we know people who feel so horribly alone, desperate, full of fear and anxiety – not knowing where to turn next; not really seeing any sign of hope for the future.

Moses, the leader of these frightened people, no doubt felt a moment of panic himself, facing that sea and hearing the impending Egyptian army in the background. He didn't know what would happen; he didn't know how they would be delivered; but he knew God was in control. He said to the people:

'Do not be afraid. Stand firm and you will see the deliverance the LORD will bring you today' (v. 13).

Then he stretched out his hand.

The seas will come. Yet God is both a God of redemption and a God of deliverance. He is Lord of all. And so, as we commence this new day, may we as God's people first stretch our hand to the Lord, in humble thankfulness, for his bountiful grace upon us; then stretch out our hand to another person, imparting to them the gift of hope, and deliverance, in Christ Jesus.

Song of the Redeemed

'The LORD is my strength and my song; he has become my salvation. He is my God, and I will praise him, my father's God, and I will exalt him' (v. 2).

For the Israelites, what had seemed so impossible became a reality. It was a miracle! The sea parted, and they were able to get safely to the other side – with the impending enemy destroyed completely. They were now safe on the far banks of the Red Sea. Delivered. It prompted worship, in the form of a song of thankfulness.

In this song they thank God for his actions, his conduct; but they also sing of his attributes, his character. What song can we sing today, which will honour God for all he has done, and for what he means to us?

The first stanza (vv. 1–12) looks backward and praises God for defeat of the enemy. It is important for us to daily confess any sins – known or unknown – then to claim victory over sin. It is not by our doing that we are forgiven, but by God's grace. As we read these words, right now, let us take a moment to pause and confess before God. Also, to give him praise for deliverance. If you know the simple little refrain, 'Thank you, Jesus', this would be a beautiful time to sing it quietly, for it is a song of the redeemed.

The second and last stanza of Moses' song (vv. 13–18) looks forward to the days that lie ahead, the anticipation and ultimate fulfilment of all God's promises and purposes for his people. Not only would this be the establishment of an earthly land of promise, but the promise of a heavenly home – for eternity – where God will reign over the redeemed of all ages. This is indeed cause for celebration! It is cause for singing a song of joy for what lies ahead, for those who believe in Christ.

As we look forward to that glorious day, feel free to sing the refrain 'Thank you, Jesus' again – replacing it with the word 'Alleluia'. For our Lord reigns. And this affirmation is worthy of singing praise to him!

James – the Ambitious One

Then the mother of Zebedee's sons came to Jesus with her sons and, kneeling down, asked a favour of him (v. 20).

James and his younger brother, John, were part of the first group of disciples called by Jesus – along with Andrew and Peter. James was the son of Zebedee, the fisherman. It's recorded that when Jesus called, the two brothers immediately left their boat, and their father, and followed him (Matthew 4:22). We don't learn too much in Scripture about the families or parents of the disciples. But in this case, we do learn something about James's mother. She was ambitious for her sons. And her ambition seems to have transferred to her offspring.

All mothers want the very best for their children; but usually not at the expense of others. At least not overtly. Zebedee's wife was different. At a certain point in Jesus' ministry she went, with her two adult sons, and made a request: that both James and John sit in heaven on either side of Jesus. Pretty bold! An extremely assertive and forceful woman. In Mark's Gospel it is recorded that it was James and his brother who made this same request (10:35–37). Driven people! Very forthright indeed. The ambition had rubbed off – and especially, we note, with James.

Following the request, Jesus asked them if they were prepared to drink from the cup from which he was about to drink. They readily said they were; yet he was referring to the cup of suffering. James did not know what he was affirming, for he wasn't even at the cross when needed most. He deserted Christ at the crucial moment in time. His selfish ambition turned to fear.

However, we know that it all eventually touched his heart – deeply. He knew intuitively what Jesus went through, for his sake: the pain, the agony, the suffering. All for him, and for the world at large. James eventually did come to taste of that bitter cup, for he was the first disciple to give his life as a martyr, killed by the sword of Herod. All self-centred ambition . . . gone. Yes, his life was to be all for Jesus!

James – My Redemptive Story

When the disciples James and John saw this, they asked, 'Lord, do you want us to call fire down from heaven to destroy them?' (v. 54).

Jesus gave us the name 'Boanerges', which means 'Sons of Thunder'. It was a correct name for me, no question; but not as much so for my brother, John as he was more gentle by nature. I suppose I could blame it on the temperament of my father, Zebedee. But I believe too many of us do this – blame our faults, our negative personality traits, on our parents. Aren't we all responsible for our own actions – and reactions to people and situations?

I went right away when called by Jesus to follow him. It seemed like a good move, and opportunity. For he was becoming popular and I wanted to do something different with my life, other than just fishing. You know the story of my mother, asking if we could sit on either side of Jesus in heaven. I actually spurred her on to do this. Yes, she wanted the best for her sons. But I desperately wanted to be noticed, and recognised; to be prominent. At the end, it was my mother who was at the cross, being there for Jesus, not me. How pathetic is that – after being constantly by his side for three years?

One day, when the Samaritans had not welcomed all of us when approaching their territory, I immediately thought of Elijah calling down fire from heaven. So I suggested to Jesus that we destroy them all in similar fashion. How arrogant and cruel! And me, a disciple?

But, thank the Lord, a complete change finally took place within me; sadly, not until after Christ's death and resurrection. Because of all that took place I knew, beyond all doubt, that I had been redeemed, changed, transformed, made clean. It was then that I was more than willing to drink the cup of suffering Christ spoke about, if necessary, for his sake. I was willing to give my very life for him.

For, praise be to him, I had been redeemed – by the blood of the Lamb!

The Right Attitude

Be merciful to me, LORD, for I am faint; O LORD, heal me, for my bones are in agony. My soul is in anguish. How long, O LORD, how long? (vv. 2, 3).

This penitential psalm of David is a cry to God for help. It's an acknowledgment of a deep need – for God to come and show mercy; to bring healing and restoration. Things can suddenly be taken from us: our money, our jobs, our health, our homes, our loved ones, our dignity. Nothing is a guarantee. But one thing that cannot be taken from us is our attitude, how we respond to our losses. It's up to us.

Once we sincerely pray to have a right attitude in life, we are then able to pray for others – to reach out beyond ourselves to a hurting world; to help people embrace right attitudes toward life, no matter what circumstances they are facing. Mother Teresa had a beautiful attitude toward life, while working latterly in the gutters of Calcutta. The following is an excerpt from a prayer attributed to her:

O God, we pray for all those in our world who are suffering from injustice: For those who are discriminated against because of their race, colour or religion; For those imprisoned for working for the relief of oppression . . . For those suffering from hunger and famine; For those too weak to help themselves . . . Forgive us, Lord, if we unwittingly share in the conditions or in a system that perpetuates injustice. Show us how we can serve your children and make your love practical by washing their feet. Amen.

It is having an attitude that goes beyond self. An attitude that is right, and lifts us above our own personal suffering and difficulty. It projects outward, and upward. The psalmist concludes:

The LORD has heard my cry for mercy; the LORD accepts my prayer (v. 9).

Let us embrace an attitude of love, of grace, as we reach out in prayer, and in practical ways, to a needy world.

Morning Has Broken

This is the day the LORD has made; let us rejoice and be glad in it (v. 24).

> Morning has broken Like the first morning,
> Blackbird has spoken Like the first bird.
> Praise for the singing! Praise for the morning!
> Praise for them, springing Fresh from the Word!
> *(SASB 35)*

This popular Christian hymn, first published in 1931, was written by the English poet Eleanor Farjeon. She had been asked to write a hymn giving thanks for each new day, to be set to the beautiful Gaelic tune 'Bunessan'. It has now become a classic, a jewel, lifting our spirits at the beginning of a brand new day.

We are to be glad, to rejoice and give thanks, always, for each day.

> Sweet the rain's new fall Sunlit from Heaven,
> Like the first dewfall On the first grass.
> Praise for the sweetness Of the wet garden,
> Sprung in completeness Where his feet pass.

The imagery of the rain being 'sunlit' from heaven stirs our hearts; for as it falls on the grass, bringing sweetness to the garden, we see the completeness of God's creation. The sun, rain, flowers, dew – the majesty of it all! And it is then that we see the handprint of Jesus on what he has made for us. It's all mine – and it's all yours!

> Mine is the sunlight, Mine is the morning,
> Born of the one light Eden saw play.
> Praise with elation, Praise every morning,
> God's re-creation Of the new day!

I trust you are singing this song to yourself, or even out loud – joining your voice with many others around our world today!

Daily Bread

The LORD said to Moses, 'I will rain down bread from heaven for you.
The people are to go out each day and gather enough for that day. In this
way I will test them and see whether they will follow my instructions'
(v. 4).

What would life be like without bread? Perhaps you have had some already today; or you are still waiting in anticipation. Maybe at noon you will have more; and at the evening meal, it adds something special to what already is being served. It is a main staple for many – and enjoyed by most.

The bread, or manna, spoken of in this passage was about food and sustenance. But it was even more so about dependence upon God. Food was provided in this way for only one day at a time – a test to see if the people would live by faith, trusting him for his power and deliverance. The bread was a sign of the very presence of God. He was with them, and would never forsake them. For if they held on to their faith, God would provide them with this promise:

'In the morning you will see the glory of the LORD' (v. 7).

Several things come to mind when reading this passage. First, one cannot help but reflect upon the Lord's Prayer: 'Give us this day our daily bread.' So often we take things for granted – especially those who live in wealthier countries. Let us be aware, today, of our total dependence upon God in all things. The sun and rain, the elements, are not in our hands. Virtually, all bread *is* from heaven.

Second, spiritual food is as necessary to life itself as physical food is – and even more so. Daily, we must feast on his Word. Daily, we must commune with God in prayer. Daily, we must use and exercise our faith.

Third, we must think beyond ourselves to people who have far less than we do. What can we do to make a difference? God will reveal, if we are open to him.

Let us anticipate and be thankful for the daily bread, the manna, both physically and spiritually. And let us pray for others today, that God will show himself to them in a profound way.

Water

'I will stand there before you by the rock at Horeb. Strike the rock, and water will come out of it for the people to drink' (v. 6).

Water. Clean, pure water. It's a necessity of life. But easier said than done. These days we have oil spills, water contamination in cities, sanitary issues in communities. It affects plant life, animal life, human life. We need good water. Yet now it is becoming a major issue and concern worldwide.

Backtrack thousands of years to the newly formed Israelite nation, wandering in the desert. The people, the little children, the livestock were all thirsty. They desperately needed water. They turned to their leader. Where was Moses to find it? The children of Israel were so despondent that they were ready to stone Moses.

Then God spoke. He told Moses to go to the rock at Horeb, take his staff, then strike the rock. Water would come. It would be a miraculously produced abundant supply of life-giving water. Enough for three million people, and all their livestock. It came. And it met the need. The rock Moses struck is a type of Christ, as referred to in 1 Corinthians:

They drank from the spiritual rock that accompanied them, and that rock was Christ (10:4).

They were able to find more than enough water for the next forty years. Similarly, no mere trickle of redemption flows from the cross. It is a supply abundant enough to save and to keep. Water. Pure, holy water. Water that gives life. Christ, our Rock of Ages, has a standing invitation:

Whoever is thirsty, let him come; and whoever wishes, let him take the free gift of the water of life (Revelation 22:17).

Thought

Let us be conscious of water today. As we see it, drink it, let us be extremely thankful for it. Pray that all people will find sustenance this day, physically and spiritually.

Call from a Mountain

'You will be for me a kingdom of priests and a holy nation' (v. 6).

In the previous chapter (18), Moses' father-in-law gave him good advice. Jethro was concerned for Moses' physical and mental health, for he was doing all the work himself. What resulted was the political organisation of Israel as a nation. Now they were ready to be given *spiritual* organisation in the giving of the Ten Commandments at Mount Sinai. But the Israelites needed to be spiritually prepared, in order to receive from God. This was true for Moses; and it was true for the people themselves.

For Moses, the Lord called to him from the mountain. It was a personal and direct call. We have to remember all he had been through: his years in Egypt, the murder of an Egyptian, the forty years away, back to Egypt again with Pharaoh and then the grumbling people, his deep feelings of inadequacy, and his questioning heart through it all. Yet God was preparing him.

Francis Thompson says in the famous poem, 'The Hound of Heaven', that the heart of religious experience is the fact that God seeks us, not that we seek him. It is God who takes the initiative, as he did here with Moses. How extraordinary – that God would seek out you and me! Moses comes to this realisation, that he is being called, and therefore equipped. This seals his commitment.

The people also were made fully aware of God's love and commitment to them. He reminds them that God carried them out of Egypt *'on eagles' wings'* (v. 4), and brought them *'to myself'* (v. 4). How intimate! He then speaks of the priesthood of all believers: *'You will be for me a kingdom of priests'* (v. 6).

But first, before anything else, they must consecrate themselves. They were to live holy lives, pure lives, lives pleasing to God. A life of holiness.

Prayer

Today, O Lord, I consecrate myself once again to you. Help me to live a life of holiness, a life that is pleasing and acceptable to you.

Let Justice Prevail

'For I the LORD *love justice, I hate robbery and wrongdoing' (v. 8, NRSV).*

Tomorrow is the World Day of Prayer, and people from around the world will gather together to pray. All denominations, races and cultures will join together with one goal. It's a beautiful thing, really. This worldwide prayer initiative, which has been in existence since the nineteenth century, is observed in over 170 countries. It commenced as a women's movement; yet, in recent years more men have seen the great value in united prayer.

The theme for this year is 'Let Justice Prevail', prepared by the people of Malaysia. What an important subject for a unified prayer focus in our present age, for there are so many injustices taking place in our world: against women, against children, against the poor, against the marginalised and victimised.

There is such strength in knowing that tomorrow people will be gathered all around the globe – praying for social justice. If we truly believe in the power of prayer, then we believe God will indeed both listen to and answer our prayers. We are all one in the Spirit, praying together. It helps us to affirm our faith together in Christ as we share various needs and concerns.

This worldwide day of prayer also makes the world smaller somehow. We do not have to live in isolation from one another. We can pray, together. We can all help to carry one another's burdens: to think of the poor, the afflicted, the imprisoned, the broken, the oppressed, the ones who feel so abandoned in society.

It is an international, ecumenical expression of love, unity, oneness. Let us be in prayer, today, for tomorrow's World Day of Prayer – that it will be meaningful and significant. Indeed, that justice *will* prevail in our world!

Prayer

Lord, today I pray for justice in our world. Help me, in some way, to be an active participant – so people around the world can experience complete freedom in you.

United in Prayer

Make every effort to keep the unity of the Spirit through the bond of peace (v. 3).

Today, people around the world are assembling to pray. Perhaps you are planning to participate in what the people of Malaysia have carefully prepared – to aid us all in our prayers. The prayers are for the needs of Malaysia, yes; but also the needs around the world as it relates to social justice. Even if it is not possible for us to link in with a World Day of Prayer service, this does not stop us from praying for these critical issues. We can all still be joined together in prayer. And so, how can we pray in a meaningful way?

Pray for victimised women. Many are used, and abused. Some are sexually trafficked. Some have absolutely no freedom. Many are oppressed, even imprisoned in their own home environment. Pray that they will experience freedom and liberty in Christ.

Pray for abused children. Children are gifts from God. Yet many people see them as easy targets for exploitation, things that are not of God. Pray that these children will find safety and security. Pray that they will find people they can trust. Pray they will experience freedom in their innocence, and know God truly loves them.

Pray for the developing world. People need to open their hearts to give financial aid. But even more than this; people need to be willing to walk beside, and be available to help wherever and whenever needed – in whatever capacity that is required.

Pray for unity. We are one in the Spirit, one in the Lord. We sing about this, but we also need to live it out in practical ways; to be there for one another. Unity is crucial for moving forward.

Finally, let us commit to praying continually for one another – in order to bring peace and justice on earth. Let it begin with me.

Prayer

O God, today – with so many others – I pray for justice in our world. Let justice prevail! And may I daily continue to pray for freedom in your Son, Jesus Christ, for *all* people.

A Prayer for Justice

O LORD my God, in thee do I take refuge; save me from all my pursuers, and deliver me (v. 1, RSV).

We have just experienced the World Day of Prayer, with the theme focused upon 'justice'. This psalm of David is also all about justice, and the desire of one's heart for it to indeed prevail. The 'Cush', a Benjamite, referred to in the introduction to this psalm, remains a mystery, since this name is not mentioned as a contemporary of David in the Bible. Some feel it could be another name for Shimei (2 Samuel 16:5; 9:16), the Benjamite who not only cursed David but also threw rocks at him during David's hasty retreat from Jerusalem after Absalom's revolt.

David knew that God was the supreme Judge and that, if he was patient in his prayers, the right and perfect outcome would take place – for God was impartial, and fair; a God of justice. He was both supreme and trustworthy:

Awake, my God; decree justice (v. 6).

David did the right thing. He could have taken things into his own hands. After all, he was a warrior. But he knew what was best for his own spirit. He wanted to be able to pray with *integrity* (v. 8) before God, and to leave it with him. He had to be patient; and this was not easy for David. But it was the right response.

There could be a 'Cush' in our own life. A person who has not treated us well. Perhaps they have attacked us physically, emotionally, spiritually. It has hurt, deeply. If we retaliate, it will no doubt be an ungodly reaction out of revenge. God asks that we take things to him in prayer, then to trust him with it all.

It's then, and then only, that we can live at peace with ourselves and the world. The psalmist fully realises this, and therefore concludes with these words:

I will give to the LORD the thanks due to his righteousness, and I will sing praise to the name of the LORD, the Most High (v. 17, RSV).

I Surrender

'Go, sell everything you have and give to the poor, and you will have treasure in heaven. Then come, follow me' (v. 21).

Surrendering everything, surrendering *all*, is easier said than done. We think it's pretty good if we surrender some; or even if we give up quite a bit. But all? Of our own free-will?

> All to Jesus I surrender, All to him I freely give;
> I will ever love and trust him, In his presence daily live.
>
> (*SASB* 474)

Can we still live in his presence, we might ask, if we don't surrender everything to him? Perhaps there could be great theological debates over this one. But it really comes down to trust, and love. If we truly do love the Lord, trust him, and are truly committed to him, we will want to give him everything.

The young man in the Scripture reading today wanted to be in the presence of Jesus, to be a follower; but he was rich. Maybe not the wealthiest man in the area. But he had things he treasured; things he just couldn't part with. These things weren't bad in themselves; but when things become a priority, there is a serious issue.

Many of us are rich. No, not wealthy. But in comparison to many around us, we are indeed blessed. Judson van de Venter, who wrote the words of this great song over 100 years ago, struggled with either working at and developing his natural artistic abilities, to possibly become somewhat famous and rich, or giving everything over to Jesus – surrendering his entire life to him. He chose the latter, then penned the words of this hymn.

They pick up from Peter's response to Jesus, following the encounter with the rich young ruler, who finally turned away: *'We have left everything to follow you!'* (v. 28). May it also be our response to him, today.

> I surrender all, I surrender all.
> All to thee, my blessèd Saviour, I surrender all.
>
> (refrain)

First of the Ten Great Commandments

'You shall have no other gods before me' (v. 3).

God's moral laws are absolute. When we start messing with them we not only fail ourselves but our families are affected, the church suffers, and the community in which we live begins to disintegrate. It's a definite ripple effect. And so, we should listen very carefully to God's Word – and in this case, the Ten Commandments. They were important when they were written; they are still both crucial and vital for today.

The first commandment, of course, is paramount. God is God. '*I AM WHO I AM*' (*Exodus 3:14*). He alone is to be worshipped. Triune God – Father, Son, Holy Spirit. If you are reading this book, you no doubt believe in God and want to draw closer to him. And yet, things may creep into our lives that pull us away from him; things that seductively lure us away from putting him foremost in our lives. We hardly notice what is happening at first. We don't see these various 'activities' hindering our walk with God. But then we notice that our devotional time is becoming shorter, or sometimes non-existent. Our intimate communion with him seldom happens. Other 'gods' have crept in – suffocating us, bringing us down.

It can be something as simple as TV, or certain 'toys' we possess. It can be clothes we wear, or the want for more money in the bank. It can be our job, our family. Anything that takes priority over God is detrimental to our spiritual life. God is to come first – always.

Putting God above all is the key to our existence. It's the basis of our worship. It is the sole foundation for all things. It demands an absolute single-heartedness. And so I close today, thinking of this first and most important commandment, with a Franciscan blessing for each one of us. May it inspire us, move us, touch us:

> And the blessing of God the Supreme Majesty and our Creator,
> Jesus Christ the Incarnate Word who is our Brother and Saviour,
> And the Holy Spirit, our Advocate and Guide, be with you
> And remain with you, this day and forever more. Amen.

Imagine

'Therefore since we are God's offspring, we should not think that the divine being is like gold or silver or stone – an image made by man's design and skill' (v. 29).

The second commandment speaks of having no idols, no *graven* images. For the people then, it meant not bowing down to idols – like the golden calf. But what does it mean for us today? It means not worshipping money or people; not worshipping sex or pornography; not worshipping power or the desire for it. Any of these things can be so damaging and detrimental.

Our allegiance is to be directed toward God alone. To worship him with complete abandonment. Rather than worship an *image*, let us begin to *imagine* what wonders he will do – in and through us. To imagine what it will be like, one day, to worship him – day in and day out. A popular worship song with this same title, *Imagine*, gives to us a glimpse of what lies ahead for each of us:

> I can only imagine what it will be like
> When I walk by Your side
> I can only imagine what my eyes will see
> When Your face is before me
> I can only imagine.[5]

Who needs an image to worship, of any kind, when we can have communion with the Creator? To bask in his presence! For our aim in life should only be to honour, praise and glorify him; lifting up his name with joy in our hearts. One day, we will be with him. What will it be like? How will we react? The refrain of *Imagine* says it all:

> Surrounded by Your glory, what will my heart feel?
> Will I dance for You, Jesus, or in awe of You be still?
> Will I stand in Your presence or to my knees will I fall?
> Will I sing 'Hallelujah', will I be able to speak at all?
> I can only imagine, I can only imagine.

God's Holy Name

For this is what the high and lofty One says – he who lives forever, whose name is holy (v. 15).

We are told in the third commandment not to *misuse* (NIV) the name of God when we speak. What does this really mean for us? We might think this particular commandment doesn't really apply to us, because we don't use God's name in a profane way. We don't swear, or use terrible language. So, are we off the hook here?

We certainly hear God's name misused all around us – in the various cultures in which we live. And offensive language disturbs us – even making us cringe at times. It's blasphemy, really; a disrespect and antagonism toward God. For it was God, in the beginning, who gave to us the gift of language and of speech. It's a verbal rebellion against him, when people use his name in a flippant way; or further still, language in a distasteful manner.

But also when we use language to hurt others, it grieves not only the person to whom it is directed, but it deeply wounds God as well. For they are men, women and children whom he has created; each one made in his image. When we stab others with our hate-felt words, we do not bring glory to God's holy name. To destroy relationships, even temporarily, is to destroy what God has made for us to enjoy. His name has been attacked, even if indirectly, and thus all are affected. The splendour of God the Creator has been tarnished by harsh and destructive words toward another – and therefore toward God himself.

The tongue can be used for great and glorious words of edification and encouragement; but it can also be used to cut, to damage, to destroy. This same tongue can, in fact, be blasphemous toward God's name by being on fire in a sinful, damaging way.

In all we say today – relating to both God and others – may we give both reverence and respect. In our conversation, even in an attempt to use humour, may everything said be God-glorifying. May we lift up the holy name of God by honouring him, in all we say and do.

James – the Unknown Disciple

Those who had been scattered preached the word wherever they went (v. 4).

We are told that James was the son of Alphaeus. But unlike James, the son of Zebedee, brother of John, we know virtually nothing about this James. However, we do know that he was chosen. For he was one of the twelve. Perhaps he could be referred to as a representative of all the unknown people who have followed Christ; those who have sought to spread the word of Christ to others.

In the book of Acts, we are told that believers went into the country, the world, telling others of the redemptive story of Jesus. Who were these people? What were their names? They were people like James; people who knew Christ; who knew of his death and resurrection; who knew of his great love for all people. They were not looking for fame; but wanted to spread the good news – out of a personal conviction.

James symbolises all those who have gone before us. Names we do not know; many who have given their lives for Jesus' sake. Some would say that James was a 'nobody'. But not so. He was one of the twelve. Christ chose James because of his character, his potential. Christ chooses us because we are unique. We are needed by God for his mission. Chosen, because he loves us that much.

James's title should really be changed. Not simply James, son of Alphaeus; nor James, the unknown disciple. But instead, James, child of God; or James, chosen by Jesus!

What about us? Do we ever wonder what we're doing for Christ? Or do we ever wonder about our own identity and significance? Think of an atom. We can't even see it – so insignificant, we might think. Yet there is enough power in the atoms of a thimbleful of water to drive an ocean liner for thousands and thousands of kilometres or miles. We can't even begin to fathom it all.

Let us be a humble people; yet still embracing the confidence and assurance that we are indeed chosen – enabling us to go out and change the world, for Christ's sake.

James – My Magnificent Story

Rejoice that your names are written in heaven (v. 20).

No doubt you have skipped by my name many times. Or you have thought I was James, the brother of John, son of Zebedee. That's not me. That James is a great and wonderful person. But it's not me. I've struggled with this; but I'm OK with it now. For I know Jesus also called me. And he called me for a reason. We all have great worth and significance. We all have value and importance – all in different kinds of ways.

I am here to simply tell you we are all chosen by God. We all have a definite purpose in life. We may question: Why am I here, and he's there? Why has this happened to me, and not to her? What can I really offer? Or why haven't people noticed what I do? If I slipped away, would anyone really notice?

Why do we do this kind of 'stinking thinking', as someone blatantly put it? I guess it's human nature. But it's false and a corrupted way of thinking. Jesus would surely notice, if no one else, if we didn't show up. Yes; we often struggle with identity issues. But we shouldn't, if we are to honour Christ.

We do have great purpose; for we are all disciples of Christ. I had to be reminded of that many times. And I needed to especially be reminded that my name is in the Book of Life. Not as a big, important, well-known person in the eyes of the world. But a very important person in the eyes and heart of God himself.

In a very wonderful way, I was so privileged to be *with* Jesus, every day. To witness, with my own eyes, the healings; the way he cast out demons; the way he was with children. I was there when he walked on water, cleansed the temple, fed the multitudes. I saw him hang on that cruel cross. But I was also there to witness his glorious resurrection and ascension! And yes; he is still alive today.

Let us stop thinking about what we could have been, and take great joy in what we are, and who we are becoming in Christ. One day, we will all see our names written in that Book of Life. For we are known, and cherished, by the Creator of the universe!

Majesty of God

What is man that you are mindful of him, the son of man that you care for him? (v. 4).

Tomorrow marks the birthday of my daughter, Rochelle – my firstborn. To this very day I can still relive the experience of her birth (extremely painful!); but then, the first glimpse of her. Perfectly formed. Her tiny little fingers, her beautiful little toes (and yes, I quickly counted, to make sure there were ten!). As the tears flowed down my face, very early that Saturday morning, I thanked God for her safe arrival. I thanked him, in all his awesome majesty.

'How majestic is your name!' David exclaimed (v. 1). It must have been one of those moments for him also; a moment when he was so full of praise and thankfulness, simply overwhelmed by God's creative power. As he looked up to the heavens, he couldn't believe what he saw – in all its glory. NASA tells us that the Hubble space telescope has observed 3,000 billion galaxies. Mind-boggling!

The birth of a tiny baby. Billions upon billions of galaxies. 'O LORD, our LORD . . .' Awe. Wonder. Glory. How great thou art! Yet the psalmist doesn't just speak of God's creative power. He brings everything into focus when he speaks of our identity in him:

You made him a little lower than the heavenly beings and crowned him with glory and honour (v. 5).

Who are we, in Christ? Who are we, in relation to this vast universe? How do we fit into God's plan? Why should God be mindful of you and me? Some might toss it off, saying we are mere accidents – no meaning, no purpose. But the psalmist goes on to clarify his questions, by actually answering them. We are *all* 'crowned' with glory – by God himself! He loves us that much. And with this, giving us all respect, dignity, 'honour'.

This magnificent psalm ends with a doxology, which is actually an affirmation of the opening statement. May it be our verse for today:

O LORD, our LORD, how majestic is your name in all the earth! (v. 9).

Near the Cross

May I never boast except in the cross of our Lord Jesus Christ, through which the world has been crucified to me, and I to the world (v. 14).

Fanny Crosby became blind at the age of six weeks, from maltreatment of her eyes. Growing up she never complained, was educated well, and eventually became a teacher. Fanny loved writing poetry, then started writing hymns – more than 4,000 of them! She married and was very happy, despite her disability.

Her philosophy of life was that if it had not been for her affliction, she might not have had such a wonderful influence upon other hymnwriters. Also, she had such a magnificent memory. Before she was ten, she had memorised the first four books of the Old Testament and the four Gospels. Incredible!

The beautiful and well-known hymn, 'Near the Cross', draws us closer to Calvary. It reminds us of the significance of the cross, and the need to have it ever before us:

> Jesus, keep me near the cross;
> There a precious fountain,
> Free to all, a healing stream,
> Flows from Calvary's mountain.
> (*SASB* 115)

The imagery of the fountain and stream, flowing for us, is not only stunning but also captivating. It is precious, to be treasured. Paul reminds us that we are not to boast about what we have, or what we've accomplished in life, but to boast only in the cross: to see the cross as our healing stream; to see the cross as what life on Earth is all about. Then, to walk daily in the shadow of the cross – in all we say and do.

For each of us, may this be our constant prayer.

> Near the cross! O Lamb of God,
> Bring its scenes before me;
> Help me walk from day to day
> With its shadow o'er me.
> (v. 3)

Holy Day

'If you keep your feet from breaking the Sabbath . . . if you call the Sabbath a delight . . . then you will find your joy in the LORD' (vv. 13, 14).

The fourth commandment speaks to keeping the Sabbath day holy. For Christians, this usually means Sunday – yet really it could be any day of the week. Most of us attend church on Sunday, and usually anticipate this day to focus on God Almighty. Sometimes, however, we come to think of this day as being drawn out, even boring at times; a day that is extremely busy, and sometimes dreaded by children – with various restrictions placed on this day by parental authority.

This Sabbath day should be a time for rejoicing; a day that is celebrated because it gives meaning to life. It gives meaning to our relationship with God, and all other significant relationships in our life – family, friends, community. On this special day, we are reminded – as it is set apart – that there is more to life than our job, going to movies, eating at a restaurant, working and labouring. It's a time to rediscover God in a new and exciting way. It's a day set aside to spend quality time with extended family. It's a holy day, as we encourage one another. It's a day of thanksgiving.

It's a day to rest. Some question this, as we often find ourselves so busy on this special day – teaching, preaching, giving, preparing. Our minds sometimes go in all directions, for it's often a hectic day for Christians! Yet we are speaking of a different kind of rest here. It's to enjoy intimate communion with the Saviour. It's making sure the day is held sacred, and holy. It's allowing Jesus to minister to us, in the quietness. It's a rest from the ordinary, the routine. It's setting aside things we do on other days – to adore and honour the Lord.

Perhaps it would do us no harm to re-evaluate what we do with this holy Sabbath, this holy day – seeing if any adjustments need to be made in our household. For, when we completely focus on God alone, it will bring a deep inner joy like nothing else. Our hearts are then in tune with his – and nothing can compare!

Honouring our Parents

'Honour your father and your mother, as the LORD your God has commanded you' (v. 16).

The family unit is the very core of society. When this fabric is strong, the society around it becomes stronger. Yet, as we are all fully aware, the *idea* of the family unit as being fundamental is disintegrating in many parts of our world. We don't even know how to define 'family' any longer; and it's mostly to do with selfishness and a complete lack of focus and reverence toward God.

This dissipation of the family unit usually begins with a lack of respect and honour toward parents. People seem to read this particular commandment – to honour our mother and father – as taking away from the cult of individualism. Children think *they* are the ones to be honoured; adults blame *their* parents for everything that's gone wrong in their lives.

True, there are many pressures placed upon all of us today. But many cultures oppose discipline, in any form. They feel moral sanctions take away from freedom of self-exploration. Children want to express who they are, whenever they want, and in whatever way they choose. As adults, we often feel older parents didn't know what they were doing. Authority, and respect for it, is often no longer part of our mindset.

However, is it all about our needs and our wants? Is this how a society is built – to be strong and influential? In some cultures parents *are* highly respected and honoured. And this is good. But in other places this has gone by the wayside. People, no matter what age, often think they have all the answers to life's questions and situations. Wisdom is not sought and treasured.

We would be wise to look again at this fifth commandment. Today, let us pray for the family. Let us pray for fathers and mothers, that they will be wise parents. Let us pray for children (which includes all of us!) that we will be respectful and honouring. Finally, let us love and respect our elders – and in so doing, give honour to God, our heavenly Father.

Love of Life

Now choose life, so that you and your children may live and that you may love the LORD your God (vv. 19, 20).

We are told in this sixth commandment not to kill. Ah . . . some final relief, we think, because we'd never contemplate murder! However, we are quickly reminded of Jesus' Sermon on the Mount in which he says we are not to be angry with another – for such persons are liable to judgment. Most of us are suddenly in deep trouble here; for most of us have been angry with someone – and often a person very close to us. So, how can we understand this?

It's all about what's going on inside. Obviously, a murder can be proven in a court of law. But anger begins internally, and often festers. It can start to tear us apart, for it can soon turn to hatred. It can consume us. What's the answer then to this strong emotion which can take over our whole being?

Love. Sounds simple, doesn't it? But love is really the only viable answer, the only possible antidote for anger and hatred. It's about reconciliation. It's about forgiveness. It's about the love of life itself – ours, and the life of another. Yet what if the person doesn't deserve to be forgiven; or we really don't want to be reconciled? Well, what if God took this line of thinking with us? A different story – yet the same story, really.

The love of life speaks to our purpose, the meaning for our existence. Do we enjoy living, thanking God daily for life itself? If yes, then we must seek out someone, and in so doing thank God for that person's life. We must see their great potential, their value, their giftings, their positive qualities. Then, we must reach out in love and, in so doing, show them the love of life we possess. It requires humility, and a contrite heart. It requires God's love.

Prayer

Lord, forgive me for any hatred or anger I may be harbouring. Cleanse me, through and through. And help me to really love others, as you love me.

John – the Beloved

'But I am giving you a new command. You must love each other, just as I have loved you' (v. 34, CEV).

When we think of the disciple John, words come to mind such as warm, gentle, loving, kind, affectionate, soft-spoken, spiritual. After all, he is referred to as the 'beloved' disciple; the one, perhaps, closest to Jesus. But he wasn't always like this. He was once a fisherman, after all; and he was referred to by Jesus, along with his brother James, as 'sons of thunder' (Mark 3:17). For John once had a temper. He'd flare up when things annoyed him. He was very much on the edge, quick to react, even somewhat volatile at times.

He had come a long way from his sectarian, rather prejudiced attitudes. Mark records for us an incident when someone was driving out demons in Christ's name (see 9:38–41). This was a new believer who was only trying to help a man in desperate need by calling on Christ's authoritative power. But he was not one of the twelve; and John didn't like this, at all. In John's opinion, this believer was not important enough to perform such a miracle. So he told the man to stop.

Jesus rebuked John for doing this; for there was no such thing as a certain *class* of believers. One believer is no more prominent than another. Jesus went on to say that anyone who even gives a cup of cold water to someone, in Christ's name, is doing the right thing. All are equal before the cross of Christ.

So what changed this rather temperamental, prejudiced, sometimes hot-tempered man into an endearing 'beloved' disciple? Love. A simple answer. Yet, as simple as it seems, it carries profound depth. Just before Christ's impending sacrifice and death, he gathered the twelve to his side. He told them he'd soon be leaving them – and it would be up to them to spread the good news about Christ. There would only be one way people would identify them as followers; and that was to *love* one another. John took this very much to heart. He loved, from the inside out.

We are to do likewise. And so, today, let us love well.

John – My Beautiful Story

One of them, the disciple whom Jesus loved, was reclining next to him (v. 23).

I was an ordinary guy, with ordinary traits – some good, some not so good. I had goals, dreams, thoughts of what I'd like to do with my life. Then, in one day, everything changed. I was listening to John the Baptist preach. He had been questioned about whether or not he was the prophet. John went on to speak about water baptism, then spoke about something new – baptism by the Holy Spirit. He suddenly looked up at someone, and said:

'Behold the Lamb of God!' (John 1:36, NKJV).

When I saw the face of Jesus, I knew he was the Messiah – no question. I also knew my destiny was changed, right there and then. For he was not only compelling in his demeanour; Jesus was, beyond all doubt, who we'd all been waiting for.

I thought about nothing else from that day forward. I talked about him with my parents and my brother, James. I thought about him while fishing. And when he called me one day to follow him, I jumped at the opportunity. I responded immediately, for I had fallen in love with the Lamb of God.

Did my whole nature change right away? No; there was lots of refining to do. Did I show Jesus I loved him, by loving others right away? No; transformation needed to take place. But it was my deep and profound love for Christ that kept me drawing closer to him, day by day. To be near him, commune with him, hear him speak to me intimately. This is all I longed for, all I lived for.

He told all of us to keep loving him, yes; but also to love others, deeply. Sounds simple enough, doesn't it? But as you well know, sometimes it's easier said than done. Yet, if you choose to really love him, and to love others with Christ's love, you too will be called 'beloved' by Christ. Could you ask for anything more?

Call for Wisdom

For the LORD gives wisdom, and from his mouth come knowledge and understanding (v. 6).

This second chapter of Proverbs commences with two words: *My son.* These two words appear throughout the book, indicating the importance of old-fashioned virtue. They also imply the value of a strong family life, and the passing on of important life lessons from one generation to another. For the good and godly, life is to be well managed; a life that is dedicated fully to God. No matter our age or life experience, we must always be open to receiving wisdom.

If you have ever taken part in a spiritual gifts assessment exercise, wisdom is usually listed as a spiritual gift. Some might not score high on this particular gift, then conclude that it's not part of their 'gifting'. But we *all* need wisdom. It's essential for spiritual growth and development. God wants it for us.

This proverb reminds us of why the call for wisdom is so essential. Wisdom helps us to have knowledge of who God is. It helps us to keep our lives in order – for it will *enter your heart* (v. 10). Wisdom protects us from evil in the world, from making unwise decisions and choices in everyday situations. Finally, it blesses us when we adhere to godly wisdom:

Thus you will walk in the ways of good men and keep to the paths of the righteous (v. 20).

No doubt we have all made choices in life that have not been wise. Yet we learn from them, and move forward. This is the call for wisdom at work. It is a spiritual gift to be exercised, to the full.

Let us be fully aware of this gift from God. May we always call upon him to make wise decisions, for his ultimate glory.

Thought

Today, be aware of the various choices you make – in the big decisions, in the small things. Ask God to impart his wisdom to you, then give praise to him for his continual presence in your life.

Sacred Head

They stripped him and put a scarlet robe on him, and then twisted together a crown of thorns and set it on his head (vv. 28, 29).

The words of today's moving song, based on part of a Latin hymn attributed to Bernard of Clairvaux, are given to us by Paulus Gerhardt – then translated into English by James Waddel Alexander. It is interesting to note that the music, by Hans Leo Hassler, was originally composed for a secular love song. However, it marries so fittingly with this powerful hymn. Johann Sebastian Bach arranged the melody, using it five times in his *St Matthew Passion*. Thus, this wonderful hymn has come to be known as the Passion Chorale.

> O sacred head once wounded, With grief and pain weighed down,
> How scornfully surrounded With thorns, thine only crown!
> How pale art thou with anguish, With sore abuse and scorn!
> How does that visage languish, Which once was bright as morn!
>
> *(SASB 123)*

It speaks of the passion of Christ: the pain, the agony. It refers to our shame, our guilt, our sin. He bore it all – for us. This sacred head, how beautiful. All we want to do in response is to tell him how much we love him. To tell him how sorry we are for the pain we've caused. We then want to ask for his forgiveness, and to thank him for all he has done for us – and is continuing to do.

> What language shall I borrow To thank thee, dearest Friend,
> For this thy dying sorrow, Thy pity without end?
> O make me thine for ever! And should I fainting be,
> Lord, let me never, never Outlive my love to thee.
>
> *(v. 3)*

As we approach this Easter season, may the last line of the verse above ring true for each one of us. May we *always* love him, and live only for him.

Sex is Sacred

For this reason a man will leave his father and mother and be united to his wife, and they will become one flesh (v. 24).

One flesh. Union. Bonding, in every way possible. Sex is for marriage only. For marriage is to be not only a lifelong commitment, to stay together, but it's also to be a total commitment to fidelity. The seventh commandment is crucial for Christians, especially living in this present age of promiscuity. Casual and illicit relationships seem to be the norm; affairs are happening everywhere, even within the Church. People are expressing their so-called freedom in inappropriate ways – causing much grief and pain.

When a person gets married, it's because of love, of commitment. Often children come. A family unit is created. And God blesses this family. Yes, there may be tension at times, even conflict. When various personalities live under the same roof, this is bound to happen. Sometimes these arguments escalate, and some want to simply escape. Or in some cases, people get bored; life becomes routine. They want to spread their wings, try something different.

Some find their escape in doing something quite novel – a new hobby, a new form of recreation. But some seek this freedom in very dangerous places – places that eventually bring hurt, pain, destruction; not only to those directly involved, but also to all those affected by the extra-marital involvement.

God's law, his commandment, is to be upheld. It's all about being faithful to him; being faithful to our spouse. It's all about building on what we have, and remembering that the marriage is a gift from God. It's about being creative in our marriage; it's about rediscovering love; it's about making the other happy. How blessed a person is to have a partner. Such a blessing should never be taken for granted.

Challenge

Today, if married, do something very special for your spouse. If not married, or if you've lost your spouse, encourage a couple you know – and pray for them.

A Slippery Slope

'Do not murder, do not commit adultery, do not steal, do not give false testimony, honour your father and mother, and "love your neighbour as yourself"' (v. 18).

Stealing. Most would not break into another person's home, stealing their property. Most would not walk into a store, taking something without paying. However, the eighth commandment can be broken in very subtle ways. If we haven't slipped up here, we've probably at least thought about a few things – justifying those questionable thoughts in our mind; for we say to ourselves that people charge too much, take advantage of us, and don't compensate us for time spent doing various activities.

It might be a tax form we 'play' with; it might be taking a restaurant bill, using it to claim for business; it might be receiving more cash than we were supposed to receive; it could be taking a few items from work that are needed at home; it might even be taking an extra-long coffee or lunch break. You might stop here and think this has gone too far, really stretching the point. But it always starts in a small way – the beginning of a slippery slope.

People say that the downfall of Christians today is because of one of three things: power, money or sex. Three insatiable desires of our present-day culture – and perhaps all past cultures also! The want of money can be so destructive. The more people have it, the more they want. And some who don't have much will go to many extremes to get it. It mars character; it eats away at integrity; it causes anxiety, resulting in much grief. For people change, when this greed takes hold of them.

Honesty is to be greatly valued and treasured. Trust is crucial in all our dealings with people. When people know we are hard-working and trustworthy in all we do for the Lord and for others, when they know we are people of integrity, then hopefully they will see God in us – shining brightly for his glory. Today, let's be conscious of what we have, and what we don't have, and be content in our present state – thanking God for life itself.

'White' Lies

The LORD detests lying lips, but he delights in men who are truthful (v. 22).

Many societies today turn a blind eye to petty fraud and even adultery; and covetousness seems to be on the rise everywhere. But no one likes a liar. When someone lies it's an insult to both our intelligence and personhood, for that individual thinks we are not worthy of knowing the truth. Lies are an insult to our dignity as well. Then, people have the audacity to think they are only telling 'white' lies – lies that really don't count. 'White' is usually associated with goodness and purity. What could possibly be pure and good about a lie?

In saying all this, have we ever done this ourselves? Have we ever told a white lie? No doubt as a child, and usually we were caught. But what about as adults? Have we done this – to get out of a bad situation? To cover up something? To save face? Perhaps we've even tried to put the blame on someone else. Anything, to avoid repercussions.

We can only answer this for ourselves. Maybe no one even knows, to this day, something we've hidden. But God knows. And what do we do with this knowledge? A cover-up can consume us, eat us up. For there *is* no such thing as a white lie.

However, we *can* set things straight. The slate *can* be made clean. We *can* be forgiven, and move forward – in truth, and in victory. The ninth commandment, referring to false testimony, is in reference to the law. The responsibility of the judge, or jury, is to discover the truth. The truth is found in examining the character and the integrity of the witnesses. And witnesses must tell the truth, always.

Truth-telling begins at home. Parents need to be people of integrity. Otherwise their children will see right through them. Extended family are to be people of true and authentic character. Otherwise love is tarnished; love is compromised.

May we *always* uphold truthfulness as a cherished value.

Judas – the Traitor

'I tell you the truth, one of you is going to betray me' (v. 21).

He was an apostle. He started off on the right track, because he was chosen to be one of the twelve. People often depict him as the devil incarnate. But we read that Jesus prayed about his choice of apostles, for he wanted the right ones to be closest to him:

One of those days Jesus went out to a mountainside to pray, and spent the night praying to God. When morning came, he called his disciples to him and chose twelve of them, whom he also designated apostles: Simon (whom he named Peter), his brother Andrew . . . and Judas Iscariot (Luke 6:12–15).

Judas was not always dressed in black, as we often think of him. He was not always whispering behind Jesus' back. He looked and dressed like the other disciples, proclaiming the kingdom message and witnessing, like the others. For three years they all moved about together. No one seemed to question his motives, his intentions, his spiritual depth. So what happened?

Dante places Judas in the lowest hell, the *Inferno*. But he was chosen by Jesus, and no doubt felt honoured at first. When called, he gave up all to follow. But maybe things started to fester a little. You see, he was from Kerioth, the only man from the south. He would have had a southern accent. Judas might have felt awkward about this; he might have been teased, mocked, ostracised.

He hadn't been a fisherman, like many of the others; so perhaps was left out of many conversations. He was elected treasurer – quite an honour. Yet even with this position, he wasn't part of the inner circle. Perhaps there was jealousy. Things started to boil within. Then finally, when given a chance to make something for himself, in exchange for a betrayal, he jumped on it. He felt he deserved the break. One commentator put it this way: 'He followed Christ and yet took his sin with him. Thence . . . his ruin!'[6]

A follower of Christ, holding on to sin. Could it happen to us? Today, may we start by confessing all, being cleansed afresh – in order that we bask in his glorious presence, forever!

Judas – My Pathetic Story

So Judas threw the money into the temple and left. Then he went away and hanged himself (v. 5).

I started off well. Jesus simply captivated me! I somehow knew this man was a real leader and motivator. He was someone the Jewish nation needed for this moment in time. He chose me, and I accepted, for I wanted to be part of this new, dynamic movement.

But I'll be upfront and admit that I didn't seem to fit. Stuff started getting twisted in my head: jealousy of the others; envy of things they were doing, gifts they possessed; frustration, even anger, with others. My humanity, my base nature, was beginning to rule my life – and I didn't do anything to stop it.

Early on in Jesus' ministry he seemed to see right through me, which caused me to fume and fester inside. Good old John even wrote what Jesus said, so it's recorded forever:

'Have I not chosen you, the Twelve? Yet one of you is a devil!' (John 6:70).

Jesus looked right at me when he said this. Of course, I was having bad thoughts about everything. But how could he have read my mind, my heart? Another time Mary poured expensive perfume on Jesus' feet. The money could have been used to feed the poor, I said. But really, I wanted that money for myself. John records it:

He [Judas] did not say this because he cared for the poor but because he was a thief; as keeper of the money bag, he used to help himself to what was put into it (12:6).

It's true – everything. I ended up hating all of them, Jesus included. I no longer belonged, nor believed. Pathetic? You'd probably call it something far worse. Jealousy. Envy. Coveting. It grows, and festers. Let this be a warning. Take heed. It's now up to you.

Prayer

Lord, protect me, and hold me close to you – always; for I love you, with all of my heart! Make me more like you, Jesus.

Franciscan Blessing

The LORD is a refuge for the oppressed, a stronghold in times of trouble (v. 9).

This psalm of David is written for the director of music, perhaps to be sung. The psalm, or song, contains four main sections: thankfulness to God; prayers for the afflicted; appeal for God's favour; judgment of the nations. As I was contemplating these four areas of emphasis in this particular psalm, I came across a fourfold Franciscan blessing, with an added benediction. It compliments, I believe, what the psalmist is wanting to say. May it be a blessing and an encouragement to you today, as you lift your heart to God in complete adoration:

May God bless you with a restless discomfort about easy answers,
half-truths and superficial relationships, so that you may
seek truth boldly and love deep within your heart.

May God bless you with holy anger at injustice, oppression,
and exploitation of people, so that you may tirelessly work for
justice, freedom, and peace among all people.

May God bless you with the gift of tears to shed with those who suffer from
pain, rejection, starvation, or the loss of all they cherish,
so that you may reach out your hand to comfort them and transform their
pain into joy.

May God bless you with enough foolishness to believe that
you really can make a difference in this world, so that you are able,
with God's grace, to do what others claim cannot be done.

And the blessing of God the supreme Majesty and our Creator,
Jesus Christ the Incarnate Word who is our brother and Saviour,
and the Holy Spirit, our Advocate and Guide, be with you
and remain with you, this day and forevermore. Amen.

The Green Hill

They took Jesus, therefore, and He went out, bearing His own cross, to the place called the Place of a Skull, which is called in Hebrew, Golgotha (v. 17, NASB).

> There is a green hill far away, Without a city wall,
> Where the dear Lord was crucified Who died to save us all.
> (SASB 133)

The story is simple. Yet how profound! Jesus, living in order that he die, as a supreme sacrifice for us. It had to take place in order that we would have life eternal with him. Amazing!

This beautiful hymn was written actually for children, so they would understand the implications of Calvary for themselves. Cecil Frances ('Fanny') Alexander wanted even the youngest of people to know Jesus, and to take in what he has done for all of us. This hymn was placed in her book, *Hymns for Little Children*, which reached its sixty-ninth edition before the close of the nineteenth century.

> We may not know, we cannot tell What pains he had to bear;
> But we believe it was for us He hung and suffered there. (v. 2)

The hymn speaks of the deep pain Christ bore for us. It speaks of the necessity of the cross, for our forgiveness. It speaks of the desire for simply being good. It speaks of Christ's supremacy:

> There was no other good enough To pay the price of sin;
> He only could unlock the gate Of Heaven, and let us in. (v. 4)

It goes on to speak of redemption and trust. But most of all, it speaks of his great love for us. Simple. Profound. Mysterious.

> O dearly, dearly, has he loved And we must love him too,
> And trust in his redeeming blood, And try his works to do. (v. 5)

This Easter season, may these words touch our innermost being.

Words that Stick

A short series by guest writer Captain Mal Davies

Captain Mal Davies is The Salvation Army's National Editor-in-Chief in Australia as well as Territorial Literary Secretary for the Australia Southern Territory. He has a degree in English literature and writes regularly in Salvation Army magazines. He is married with two children.

His first week of devotions asks what we can learn from some simple, familiar Salvation Army choruses. Captain Davies writes:

Stored away in my jumble of a mind are the lyrics to songs and choruses that I learnt nearly forty years ago while attending Sunday school; choruses such as 'Enter, enter, right into my heart, Lord' and 'Teach me how to love thee'.

Maybe it was because we sang many of these choruses week after week, month after month and year after year that they retain a firm place in my memory banks. Or maybe it's because the truths contained in those simple lyrics were timeless, meaningful and doctrinally sound – I sang them as a child, as a teenager, as a young adult and now as a Salvation Army officer, and they continue to ring true.

Through the next week I hope to remind you of – or maybe introduce you to – some of the choruses I learnt as a child. I hope, for many of you, the tunes come readily to mind as you read the familiar words – words that still ring true year after year.

I will sing praise to my God as long as I live (Psalm 146:2).

A Heartfelt Love

May the words of my mouth and the meditation of my heart be pleasing in your sight, O LORD, my Rock and my Redeemer (v. 14).

> Enter, enter, right into my heart, Lord,
> Enter now, enter now.
> *(SASB* Chorus 64)

This is one of the first choruses I learnt in Sunday school. It's a good Sunday-school song because: first, it is easy to remember the words; second, it is repetitive, which means – like learning times tables by rote – it gets 'stuck in your head'; third, it is a song of invitation used by children at an age when we hope they would be wanting to invite Jesus into their lives.

However, why do we talk about the heart when we want Jesus to take control of our lives? When did the heart become symbolic for the whole of a person? Why do we offer our heart to the Lord?

As early as Genesis 6:5 we read that God saw human 'hearts' had become evil, and in Exodus 5–12 we read regularly of Pharaoh's 'heart' being hardened before he released the Israelites from slavery.

It seems that for millennia we have referred to the heart as the emotional, moral and spiritual core of a person's being. From Moses to Shakespeare to the Beatles, the essence of who we are is said to be based in our hearts. And I'm glad of that. It just wouldn't be the same to sing, 'Enter, enter, right into my brain, Lord'. I guess it's the way culture and literature have shaped us, but it just seems so *right* to sing about Jesus entering our heart.

I suspect it's because we don't seek only an intellectual understanding of who Jesus is – we seek a relationship with him. We don't just want to know Jesus, we want to love Jesus. And that requires giving him our hearts.

Today

Reflect upon this chorus and the Scripture reading, and again ask Jesus into your heart. Do you have an emotional connection with Jesus or only an intellectual one?

Going One Better

For in my inner being I delight in God's law (v. 22).

> Teach me how to love thee,
> Teach me how to pray,
> Teach me how to serve thee
> Better every day.
> *(SASB Chorus 105)*

In the late 1980s the corporate world began using the term 'best practice' to refer to business methods that were considered the most effective and efficient. Employees were told to be constantly on the lookout for ways their company could make money and increase their customer base. Second best wasn't good enough!

This piece of business jargon became more widespread through the 1990s as everyone from local schools to city councils to the local butchers began to urge their staff/members/participants to seek 'best practice' standards.

Think about how long you've been a Christian and then ask yourself what sort of Christian you would be if you loved, prayed and served God, as the chorus says, 'better' every day. That is, every day you live more Christlike than the preceding day. Phew! What an obligation! What a challenge! What a goal!

Is it even possible to be *constantly* improving? I don't think so. I think our flawed human nature means we will have days when we let God down, when we don't have the energy or passion to seek 'best practice' Christianity, when we know what we should be doing but we fail to do it. This, of course, doesn't mean God loves us any less, it simply affords us the opportunity to start the next day seeking to be better for him.

Imagine if the chorus said: 'Teach me how to serve thee about as well as I did today'. What sort of aim is that? We want to have a goal of 'best practice' Christianity, not 'average practice'. It's a new day in Christ – aim high!

Today

Reflect on the words of the chorus and Scripture portion and promise God to try to do your best for him.

Who . . . Me?

O LORD, you have searched me and you know me (v. 1).

> I know he cares for me, for me,
> I know he cares for me, for me;
> I'll trust my Father in heaven
> For I know that he cares for me.
> *(SASB* Chorus 133)

My wife, Tracey, has been involved in children's ministries for more than twenty years and has a genuine calling to working with young people. Beyond that, she has a degree in early childhood education and can cite the theory that supports the practice of working with children.

As we've supported each other in ministry through the years, there have been times when I've prepared a children's story for a meeting or written something for a young reader, and Tracey has reminded me of the difficulties younger children have with concepts. How do you explain to a five-year-old the notion of being 'washed in the blood of the Lamb'? Yuk!

I recall, as a child, trying to come to grips with the idea that God made the universe, knew everything, was everywhere and was even stronger than my dad. It took, indeed, a real leap of faith to believe in this God – but I could do it!

Having done that, I then had to wrap my young mind around the words of today's chorus and accept that this supreme being who ruled the universe cared for . . . me.

To be entirely honest, even as a forty-five-year-old Christian there are still times when I'm overawed by the knowledge that God cares for me. For me. For *me*. It's amazing!

I've studied theology and enjoy reading; I've heard thousands of sermons and listened to gifted speakers talk about faith; I've attended church conferences and seminars on all manner of topics. But when I feel 'lost' or overwhelmed by my responsibilities, it's this simple chorus I turn to for solace.

Today

Reflect on the chorus and Scripture and remind yourself that God's love for you is not a concept, it's a fact.

24/7/365 – I'm Yours!

Trust in the LORD with all your heart and lean not on your own understanding; in all your ways acknowledge him, and he will make your paths straight (vv. 5, 6).

> I want to live right, that God may use me
> At any time and anywhere.
>
> (*SASB* Chorus 71)

This is one of those choruses that we can sing either slowly in a prayerful manner or up-tempo with handclapping and a more boisterous approach. It's a chorus that shows flexibility and this, pleasingly, matches beautifully with what the lyrics teach. Any time. Anywhere. I want to live right so that God can use me. No restrictions or limitations or boundaries – God, I'm yours however you want me. Twenty-four hours a day, seven days a week, 365 days a year. Total flexibility and total abandonment to God's will for my life.

For seven years before becoming an officer I worked in Salvation Army programmes assisting long-term unemployed people to return to work. We would talk about occupational fields that matched people's skills and experience, and we would plot out career trajectories. We would plan where someone wanted to be in their career in a year's time, in five years, in ten and so on.

Once we had a plan in place, it was a matter of 'filling in the gaps' and doing any necessary training or study so that a person could commence their career journey from point A to B to C until, in several decades, they could retire at point H as CEO of their own company!

God doesn't do this. God says: 'I know the plan for your life. Rather than give you the whole story now, how about you just trust me and I'll make the plan happen. Do we have an understanding?'

Any time. Anywhere. I just want to live right so that God can use me.

Today

Reflect on the chorus and the Scripture, and ask if you are still open to God's leading in your life.

What? No More Words?

Surely God is my salvation; I will trust and not be afraid (v. 2).

> In thee, O Lord, do I put my trust,
> In thee, O Lord, do I put my trust,
> In thee, O Lord, do I put my trust.
> (*SASB* Chorus 73)

Stupid chorus. Couldn't the writer think of any more words? It's just the same line repeated. Sometimes we repeat the chorus and sing the exact same line six times in a row! Stupid chorus. Well, at least that's what I thought when I was ten years old. Because when you're five or six years old, you just sing whatever the Sunday-school teacher says to sing. Then, as you start to master writing and begin to think for yourself – how to write a story, how to write a poem – you get critical of other writing. You realise that some writing is good and some is not so good. Some writing you like, some writing you don't like.

So by ten, I was right on cue to decide – 'master writer' that I was – that this chorus was stupid because the writer clearly couldn't think of any other words. As I grew to a (slightly) higher level of wisdom and maturity, this chorus became very special to me. I discovered that with the repetition of the words came a focusing of my mind on Christ and a peace in my soul that indicated God was present within.

Often I can sing a line of a song in a distracted fashion or without registering the meaning of the words, but when I have to repeat the words, well . . . they become real. They bore into my mind and make me pay attention.

There is nothing in creation that is so deserving of our trust than God. There is no person, no idol, no hero, no champion, no 'god' that will love, protect and guide us as our God will. We can trust him. At all times and in all ways. We can trust him.

Today

Sing or read through the chorus several times as though God himself were sitting right in front of you, then reflect upon the Scripture.

Caught Much Lately?

'Come, follow me,' Jesus said, 'and I will make you fishers of men' (v. 17).

> I will make you fishers of men, fishers
> of men, fishers of men.
> I will make you fishers of men if you
> follow me.
>
> (*SASB* Chorus 232)

This is one of the earliest choruses I remember, although I confess this probably has more to do with the actions and imagery than the theological thrusts of the chorus. To a wide-eyed five-year-old boy, the image of Jesus standing on a shore, casting in his fishing line and catching men instead of fish was mind-boggling! It was worth becoming a follower of Jesus simply to learn how to do that.

The chorus was also fun to sing because all the boys would stand up on any word that started with 'm' and the girls on words that began with 'f'. Subsequently, the chorus was full of constant motion as people stood and sat down again, and more so if we sang it faster – which we inevitably did!

As I grew older I realised the scriptural basis for the lyrics and as I became a junior soldier, corps cadet, senior soldier, I vowed to follow Jesus and, indeed, try to win people for him and his kingdom.

These days, if I really want to honestly challenge myself, I ask: 'Have I kept this vow? Do I still want to be a "fisher of men"? Am I truly following Jesus in wanting to introduce people to God or have I become lazy in this endeavour?' I think at times it becomes easy to say: 'It's someone else's job' or 'Evangelism isn't my gifting', but the truth is that all Christians are obligated to tell others of God's love.

Are you still winning people for Christ?

Thought

As you read today's Scripture passage, note how quickly people followed Jesus. Are you quick to follow Jesus' lead – or hesitant? Recall the last person you 'caught' for Jesus, was it recently? Pray that God will give you an opportunity today to witness of your faith.

Me and God, God and Me

Thomas said to him, 'My Lord and my God!' (v. 28).

> All there is of me, Lord, all there is of me,
> Time and talents, day by day,
> All I bring to thee;
> All there is of me, Lord, all there is of me,
> On thine altar here I lay
> All there is of me.
>
> (*SASB* Chorus 34)

At times in my life it has been so hard to give all of me to God – and my focus is not so much on the word 'all' as the word 'me'. As a husband, I committed my marriage to God. As a father, I dedicated my two children to God and made solemn promises to him. When I became a Salvation Army officer I covenanted to serve God and fulfil the tasks and obligations of an officer. As a corps officer I brought people to God, with the Holy Spirit's guidance. As a writer in a Salvation Army editorial department I pray God will inspire me and use my words for his purposes.

It's easy to commit lots of things to God, including parts of my life and the gifts he has given me; but does this mean the same as 'me' to God? Apart from what I can do and how I can serve and what obligations I make, have I really given all of me to God?

I want God to have all of me: my time, talents, energy, body, mind, soul, emotions, intellect, personality, desires, attitudes, passions, commitment, private life, public life, family life, church life, spiritual life.

I want God to have me. He made me; I'm his. Without God I am nothing. It's nonsensical for me to try to be a good husband, father, brother, son, officer, neighbour or citizen without placing God first. I am what I am only because he is what he is in my life.

Lord, on thine altar here I lay . . . all there is of me.

Today

Reflect on the chorus and the Scripture, including John 1:12–13, and reconsider the relationship you have with God.

'Who Do You Say I Am?'

Guest writer Captain Mal Davies provides the series for Holy Week. In his second week of devotions, titled 'Who Do You Say I Am?', he explores several of the characters in the Passion Week story and how they may have answered this question from Jesus. Captain Davies writes:

As we move towards Easter we find, in the scriptural account of Passion Week, many people trying to identify who Jesus truly was. Was he a prophet, a mad man, a lowly carpenter, a cult leader, a liar or, indeed, the Son of God?

During our daily readings we will pose Jesus' question to the disciples – 'Who do you say I am?' – and, to several other Passion Week characters, and speculate how they might have responded.

The underlying question for us to address during this week's devotions is who we hold Jesus to be. Sure, you may have proclaimed Jesus as your Lord and Saviour when you became a Christian ten, twenty, thirty or more years ago – but does it still ring true? Is Jesus still everything to you? Do you love him as much as ever?

'But what about you?' he asked. 'Who do you say I am?' (Matthew 16:15).

No Ambiguity

'But what about you?' he asked. 'Who do you say I am?' Simon Peter answered, 'You are the Christ, the Son of the living God' (vv. 15, 16).

We live in an age of ambiguity and vagueness where, even in pockets of the Church, it seems doubt is prized above certainty. There are those who say that doctrine is 'dead' and beliefs need to ebb and flow in accordance with your own Christian journey. What's true for you today may not be next week.

Well, call me out of touch, but there are some things that should be cast in stone for all Christians. Chief among them is this identification of Jesus from his disciple Peter. I'm inclined to believe that if any Christian of any church of any denomination in the world is asked who they believe Jesus to be, they should be able to answer: 'I believe he is the Christ, the Son of the living God.'

No ambiguity. No doubt. No hesitation. No vague hope but, instead, a clear statement of truth. How can you call yourself a *Christ*ian if you don't know who Christ is?

It's the week of the Passion and our focus should be on what Jesus did for us in his trial, punishment, crucifixion and resurrection. However, these only carry any weight if we accept Jesus was someone special. If Jesus of Nazareth was just an itinerant teacher and healer then his death is bad but, ultimately, meaningless.

This week we will ask several biblical characters in the Easter story: 'Who do you say Jesus is?' As we explore their responses, I pray that you will – each day this week – ask yourself again who you believe Jesus to be.

Today

Reflect for a moment on our Scripture passage and recall when you first realised that Jesus was the Son of the living God. Has your belief changed?

The Giver of Life

The chief priests made plans to kill Lazarus as well, for on account of him many of the Jews were going over to Jesus and putting their faith in him (vv. 10, 11).

In John 12 we read of Jesus returning to Bethany to visit Mary, Martha and Lazarus. It is six days before the Passover and the day before Jesus' triumphal entry into Jerusalem.

Apart from the episode of his resurrection at Jesus' hand, we tend to not think too much about Lazarus and any further role he played in the gospel story, but this passage indicates that many people came to see Lazarus, we assume to verify the miracle of which they'd heard. It adds that 'on account of him' many people put their faith in Jesus.

Imagine being the living proof of a miracle of Jesus. Would you sign autographs? Would people want to touch you? Would you get tired of the constant stream of visitors wanting to hear the same old story?

Well, we may not have been brought back from physical death, but Jesus is responsible for reviving us from being spiritually dead. There's a sense in which each of us is another miracle of Jesus. We have new life in his name!

Who would Lazarus say Jesus is? I believe he would say Jesus is the giver of life, the reason for living and the source of eternal life. As each person who came to see Lazarus to ask if the story was true, he would let them touch him and he would say, 'Jesus is the way, the truth and – without a shadow of a doubt – the life.'

Today

Reflect for a moment on our Scripture passage and how Lazarus would have felt sitting with a man who gave him life. Thank Jesus for the new life he has given you.

A Person of Influence

Now there were some Greeks among those who went up to worship at the Feast . . . 'Sir,' they said, 'we would like to see Jesus' (vv. 20, 21).

For 2,000 years people have sought out Jesus. He has provoked discussion, piqued curiosity and caused debate more than any other figure in history. Even though more books have been written about Jesus than any other person who has walked the earth, people *still* have questions about why he is unique.

As thousands of Jews flooded into Jerusalem for the Passover festival, there were also some inquisitive Greeks who, we'll assume, did not know Israelite history and were ignorant of the prophecies of the Messiah. Nevertheless, they had heard stories of Jesus' teaching and miracles and wanted to meet him personally.

This is still the case. Even in the twenty-first century people all around the world regularly speak to Christians or visit church services to try and learn more about this man called Jesus and his claims to be one with God.

When I was a corps officer (church minister) at my first appointment, a young man – scruffily dressed and unshaven – came into my hall one day seeking a meal. I put together some lunch for him and sat and talked with him as he ate. After I had explained that he was, indeed, in a church and that I was a minister of religion, he asked: 'So who is Jesus? Tell me about him.' Christians live for this sort of invitation! I delighted in telling him of the person, purpose and power of Jesus.

Who did the Greeks say Jesus was? Even before they'd met him they knew he was a person of influence who could open their eyes to a new way of living. And he still is!

Today

Reflect for a moment on our Scripture passage and pray for the opportunity to introduce someone to Jesus. People still seek Christ – maybe through you.

Wise Teacher

. . . all the people came early in the morning to hear him at the temple (v. 38).

While studying English literature at university, in my final year I was privileged to attend two lectures on Shakespeare's *Romeo and Juliet* given by a professor who was a world-renowned expert on that play. I arrived at the first lecture to find the lecture theatre close to full rather than the usual half-full status and was told by a friend, as we took our seats, that some former students and other tutors also chose to attend this professor's lectures.

I discovered why – the lecture was brilliant! The professor provided us with some insightful comments on one of history's greatest plays.

A week later, it was time for his second lecture. It was, I confess, the only lecture in three years of university for which I woke up early and excited, and I took my seat in the lecture theatre well before time. Amazingly, the lecture was even more stunning than the first and concluded with a standing ovation for the lecturer.

In the week leading up to his crucifixion, Jesus taught at the temple each day and the crowds went there early to – I imagine – get a good seat and not miss a word from this master teacher. Do you ever get excited about learning something new from Jesus? There are times when a familiar Scripture passage suddenly comes alive with new meaning for me and I gain a fresh insight into who Jesus is. It's thrilling to learn from the Master!

Who did the crowds at the temple believe Jesus was? They believed he was a wise teacher, worthy of their attention. In the next few days, however, they would learn he was much, much more.

Today

Reflect for a moment on something you have learnt recently about Jesus, then reflect on something that God has revealed to you about yourself.

The Mystery of Jesus

Then Annas sent him, still bound, to Caiaphas the high priest (v. 24).

After praying at Gethsemane, Jesus was arrested and taken to the former, long-serving high priest Annas. Still widely respected by the Jews, it was thought that Annas might want to see this 'prophet' Jesus, who claimed to be more powerful than even the high priest himself.

Annas questions Jesus, who replies in a polite and legally correct fashion and says nothing to suggest he has breached any Jewish law. While this frustrates Annas, it is one of his guards who strikes Jesus – and this only embarrasses Annas further. After all, he is supposed to be the wise old man of Jerusalem but his questioning cannot even trap an itinerant carpenter from Nazareth! And now one of his guards has struck a man who has not yet stood trial and been found guilty of any crime.

Note also that even though he is surrounded by a detachment of Roman soldiers, Jesus is still kept bound.

So consider for a moment: Jesus does not break under interrogation from Annas; Annas keeps Jesus physically bound; Annas has no power to deal with Jesus further and send him to Caiaphas.

Who does Annas think Jesus is? Annas does not know . . . and he is afraid. You see, Annas was wise and powerful and influential. But he is suddenly shown to be ignorant, without power and without influence. He can see something different about Jesus, but he doesn't know what it is and he has no power over Jesus.

Annas was not the first person – and he won't be the last – not to know what to do with Jesus. Sometimes, based on fear of the unknown, we lash out and harm others. Today, in the ultimate act of 'lashing out', Jesus was crucified.

Today

Reflect for a moment on today's Scripture and on the quiet power Jesus showed throughout his life.

An Innocent Man

'I am innocent of this man's blood . . . It is your responsibility!' (v. 24).

I wonder how Pilate felt the day after Jesus died. Pilate was a man of considerable power and influence; a man used to being obeyed and in control. Yet the day before, he had been powerless, without influence and without control. And because of that … a man had died.

I've wondered if Pilate had a miserable Saturday ('I'm losing my power. I should have released Jesus. How could I let an innocent man die?') or a Saturday of denial ('I didn't kill him, the mob did. I made my position clear and washed my hands of his death. It was not my fault.')

Unfamiliar with Jesus' teaching, Pilate would have no inkling of what was to happen the following day; as far as he was concerned, Jesus was dead and that was the end of the matter.

Who did Pilate say Jesus was? He said he was an innocent man – and yet he allowed him to be treated like a guilty man and nailed to a cross. For maybe the first time in his adult life, what Pilate said had no influence on what actually happened.

Wherever Jesus went, there was a paradigm shift in how people lived. Social influencers were rendered powerless. The ostracised were thrust into the spotlight. Fishermen became leaders. Tax-collectors gave money away. Lepers walked. Blind men saw. Wise men were shown to be ignorant. Children were made the centre of attention.

It's Saturday, Jesus has died and has not yet risen. No-man's-land. Hiatus. A day of unfulfilled promise. A day when Pilate wandered through his palatial home lost, confused and dazed.

The world awaits Easter morn – and it doesn't know it!

Today

Can you recall a time when you were lost – physically, emotionally, mentally or spiritually – until Jesus appeared in your life? Thank him for being with you now.

A Fresh Start

But they did not believe the women, because their words seemed to them like nonsense. Peter, however, got up and ran to the tomb (vv. 11, 12).

On Easter morning, some women rose early and took spices to attend to the body of Jesus according to Jewish custom. What they found, however, was an empty tomb and some attendant angels alerting them to Christ's resurrection. The gospel account says they returned to the disciples and other followers to tell them their good news. ('Good' news? What an understatement! History's most amazing news!)

Luke's Gospel says the followers of Jesus were disbelieving and felt the words of the women were 'like nonsense'. All except Peter.

Peter – the one who had denied knowing Jesus three times and subsequently burst into tears – ran as fast as he could to the tomb. He had to see for himself that Jesus, the Christ, the Son of the living God (Matthew 16:16) was alive.

More than most, Peter craved a fresh start with Jesus. The phrase 'the gospel of the second chance' has never applied to anyone more than it has to Peter. He wanted to see Jesus again; he *needed* to see Jesus again.

Who did Peter say Jesus was? He said that Jesus was new life. Jesus was new hope. Jesus was a fresh start. Jesus was redemption. Jesus was reconciliation. Jesus was a new day.

It's Easter Sunday. Who do you say Jesus is? On this day more than any other of the year, you *must* state your position. Today is the day for clarity; today is the day for building foundations; today is the day to show your heart.

Who do you say Jesus is?

Today

Thank God for sending Jesus to give you new life. Tell Jesus who he is to you today. Answer his question: 'But what about *you*? Who do *you* say I am?'

Wanting 'Things'

The commandments, 'Do not murder', 'Do not steal', 'Do not covet', and whatever other commandment there may be, are all summed up in this one rule: 'Love your neighbor as yourself' (v. 9).

Most societies today are bombarded with advertising saying we need this, we must have that; otherwise, our life will be miserable. Or we see that our neighbour, our friend, has something good. Suddenly, we want it. It could be an item; it could be a talent. It could even be a *person* we desire. To covet something, as the tenth commandment warns us about, is to deeply want something that is not ours. This insatiable desire can take over our whole being.

Covetousness and envy create a mean spirit within. Our minds become focused on the object we want, and it can be extremely detrimental to our spiritual well-being. So what do we do to help us focus on something else, letting go of this obsession?

Perhaps it comes down to choosing a particular lifestyle that is simple. There is a set of guidelines, rules, that certain monks have adopted, and follow – which was established hundreds of years ago by a man with the name of St Benedict. He established the *Benedictine Rule* – seventy-two rules and guidelines to follow. Basically, it's living a very simplistic way of life to counter the complex world that surrounds us. When one reads through these rules, one may wonder if one could ever follow such a daily, weekly plan. It would be difficult to do, no question, outside of a monastery setting. But the idea behind it is interesting and worth reading; for it stresses a very simple lifestyle. In doing this, there is reverence for God and respect for others. It's about appreciating health, family, friends, creation, life. The blessings God has given us are to be treasured. The things we presently have are to be valued, and cherished. It's about having inner contentment.

And so this day, may we have that inner peace, that holy satisfaction, thanking God daily for the abundant blessings he has graciously bestowed upon us.

Golden Calf

When Moses approached the camp and saw the calf and the dancing, his anger burned and he threw the tablets out of his hands, breaking them to pieces at the foot of the mountain (v. 19).

Through Moses, God gave his laws to his people at Sinai. They fell into three basic categories: moral and spiritual laws (the Ten Commandments), civil and social laws, then the religious laws (which also extend into the book of Leviticus). In the chapters following the giving of the Ten Commandments, we are made aware of the details involved in the construction of the tabernacle – where God will dwell and receive his people's worship. Also, there are the specific instructions for priests, who are the chosen ones to lead worship in the tabernacle. This includes their clothing, what they must do to prepare themselves for ministry, as well as the supplies and utensils needed for worship. Even the designers and construction workers were hand-picked by God – again indicating that everyone has a purpose for their lives in God's perfect plan.

Six weeks have now passed since the people made their solemn vow of fidelity to God. Moses has not been seen since he went up the mountain to meet with God. They have concluded he died there; thus, they created a replica of an Egyptian god to worship. As Moses descends the mountain, with the newly inscribed tablets, he throws them down – dramatically proclaiming their broken covenant. After destroying the calf, he prays for Israel's repentance.

We have no doubt pictured this scene, and have questioned: 'How could God's people have done this?' But we must pause here for a moment and ask: 'Have we ever had a real valley experience?' We might not have built a calf, but what have we done when we've felt ineffective, or greatly discouraged? It's at this time that Satan attacks. Therefore, we need to look up and know that God is always there for us.

Let us never build a 'golden calf' in our life, hoping for it to bring ultimate fulfilment and pleasure. For only God, and he alone, will bring to us peace and everlasting joy.

The Tabernacle

Then the cloud covered the Tent of Meeting, and the glory of the LORD filled the tabernacle (v. 34).

The book of Exodus began, you might recall, with the sons of Jacob in Egypt. The Israelites were delivered, but then spent forty years in the wilderness. Exodus closes with the delivered people journeying toward Canaan. God has provided a tabernacle, a new place for them to dwell, as he accompanies them into Canaan.

The melody that has been heard throughout this book has been sometimes in the major key – the Israelites acknowledging their love and devotion to God. Yet often the tune shifted drastically into the minor mode, with blaring discord, as the people turned their backs on God. Yet above it all was a constant and beautiful counterpoint – God's faithfulness, God's presence, God's promise of a home one day. For he so desired to dwell in their midst.

The tabernacle was built, where he would dwell. It was built with very specific instructions, and now it was ready. This place was where they could all worship him, for he would be there.

The actual word 'worship' comes from an Anglo-Saxon word, *worthship*, which meant 'to ascribe worth or reverence' to something or someone. This word eventually became the word we have today – worship. The only Person in the world who deserves to be worshipped is God, our Lord and Saviour.

God took up residence in that tabernacle. We are told that the *glory* of the Lord filled it. How wonderful! One day, God's glory would also fill Solomon's magnificent temple. But far greater even than this is the knowledge and assurance that, today, God's Holy Spirit indwells every person who believes in Jesus Christ. How marvellous! How glorious!

Prayer

O Lord, may I be fully conscious of your indwelling presence. My body is the temple of your Holy Spirit. May I live according to this profound awareness.

Thomas – the Doubter

'Unless I see the nail marks in his hands and put my finger where the nails were, and put my hand into his side, I will not believe it' (v. 25).

He has come to be known as 'Doubting Thomas'. We even refer to people who 'question' things as a 'Doubting Thomas'. However, this does not sum up Thomas's entire personality. After all, he was chosen to be one of the twelve. Thomas had good qualities, qualities which set him apart from others. Qualities which qualified him to be a chosen apostle of Jesus Christ.

He was devout. He was an admirer of Jesus, wanting to give his life for him and his ministry. At one point, when the apostles heard that Jesus' close friend, Lazarus, had died, Jesus wanted to go back into Judea – an area that was growing more and more hostile toward him. Thomas saw the impending danger for his Lord; yet Jesus was determined. Thus, Thomas turned to the others and said:

'Let us also go, that we may die with him' (John 11:16).

It was devotion toward Jesus – to the point of possibly giving up his life for him. Yet, there was still some doubt; still some hesitation about Jesus being the Son of God. He probably tried to hide this questioning spirit; but that bit of doubt seemed to linger.

Having some doubt . . . is this always wrong? Is it always harmful? I'm sure most of us have doubts, even certain fears at times. No; doubts are not all bad. Perhaps Tennyson was simply being truthful when he wrote: 'There lives more faith in honest doubt, believe me, than half the creeds.'[7]

It's what we do with these doubts that matters. Do they shake our faith? Do we have to see, to believe? No; it's not a sin to have doubts. But there must come a time when we put it all on the line, step out in faith, and trust God with it all.

During this post-Easter period, may we not miss out on the *hope* Christ brings. May we not miss out on life itself. Rather, may we rejoice, each and every day, in Christ our risen Lord!

Thomas – My Powerful Story

Then Jesus told him, 'Because you have seen me, you have believed; blessed are those who have not seen and yet have believed' (v. 29).

There is something very important, very powerful I need to share with you. True; there has always been a shadow cast over me. And I deserved it. For my character was somewhat flawed, at the best of times. Why I ever became one of the twelve I'll never know. But I was chosen. And despite all that's been said about me, I did truly love Jesus. Ninety-five per cent of me *did* believe he was God's Son. But there was that five per cent I couldn't seem to shake.

That same five per cent always lingered at the back of my mind – even during the three years of his ministry. That nagging, sceptical feeling of doubt. Are you sure this is real, I'd ask myself? Do you have *any* doubt about his claim as being both Lord and Messiah?

I'm simply being transparent here. Maybe some people never question, nor have doubts. I think it's wonderful if people can be like this. But it just wasn't part of my DNA. I had to see things, have some kind of tangible proof, before I could really believe.

I wasn't there when Christ first came to the others, after his resurrection. I honestly didn't believe it would actually happen. I saw him perform miracles, heal the sick. But this was different.

So, here it is, what I really want and need to tell you. He knew I doubted, deep down. Therefore, a week after it all happened, Jesus appeared again. He just *appeared*! He looked right at me, right *through* me it seemed, and invited me to put my finger in his hands, and into his side. I shook all over as I touched him, in such an intimate way. I realised, beyond *all* doubt, this was real. Jesus *was* the Son of God! I responded to him in great, great humility – with tears streaming down my face: '*My Lord and my God!*' (John 20:28).

I tell you this so that you, today, will believe – with your whole being. He is alive! Jesus is God's Son, and he did everything for you and for me. Don't doubt him, ever!

The Lord is King

You hear, O LORD, the desire of the afflicted; you encourage them, and you listen to their cry (v. 17).

Certain psalms are more difficult to read. This particular psalm commences with a complaint, then goes on to speak of three different kinds of people. There is the moralist, who sits in judgment of everyone else – especially those who are rich and powerful; those who seemingly have everything going for them. Then there is the materialist, who possesses many things, always wanting more – taking advantage of everyone else because of this insatiable desire. Finally, there is the person of faith – who believes, despite all that's happening around them, that God will prevail.

Today, we find these same three groupings of people. Things have not changed. But also these same traits can often be found in each one of us, and we have to be so careful. Sometimes we find ourselves sitting in judgment of others. It can be so easy to slip into this dangerous mode of looking at others and judging their actions, their motives. Or, we can get very comfortable in our material wealth. No, it may not be wealth compared to the rich. But perhaps we are more *comfortable* than many – and sometimes neglect those who so desperately need our help.

Today, may we be like the last kind of person the psalmist describes – people of faith. To cry out, with confident affirmation:

The LORD is King for ever and ever (v. 16).

With this kind of assurance, deep-rooted in our heart, we can go through this day with joy oozing out from our heart. We can mingle with people, and they will know we are God's child because of the smile beaming on our face. Because of our faith, we embrace the assurance that God will care for the fatherless, and will watch over those who need his tender care. If he needs us to be his hands and his feet, may we be ready and willing; for he is our King – now, and for always.

Thine is the Glory

But thanks be to God, who always leads us in triumphal procession in Christ and through us spreads everywhere the fragrance of the knowledge of him (v. 14).

The French hymn 'Thine is the Glory', written in 1885 by Edmond L. Budry, is both glorious and triumphant in its proclamation of the risen Christ:

> Thine is the glory, Risen, conquering Son;
> Endless is the victory Thou o'er death hast won.
> *(SASB 152)*

We have just come through another Easter experience – and so we sing with confidence and assurance. The 'fear and gloom' of Good Friday is gone and we, as Christ's Church, his people, are to sing hymns such as this 'with gladness' for 'death has lost its sting'.

The third verse of this great song of triumph commences with a curious line:

> No more we doubt thee, Glorious Prince of Life!

Doubts sometimes do come. Perhaps not doubts about God's existence – although this can happen – but doubts that creep into our mind, into our life, when things don't happen as we anticipate. Such as when people are not healed; when family members are not saved; when death comes suddenly for someone; when someone betrays us. We might ask, 'Where is God when we need him the most?'

He is there, right with us! He knows all about pain, suffering, agony, betrayal, abuse, abandonment. And because of this, because of his wonderful victory over it all, he will see us through to the very end – and help us conquer *all* of life's difficulties.

Do you believe this? The victory *is* endless!

> Make us more than conqu'rors Through thy deathless love;
> Bring us safe through Jordan To thy home above. (v. 3)

The Emerging Generation

The LORD your God has blessed you (v. 7).

The book of Deuteronomy, or 'second law', is a review of the forty-year period the Israelites spent in the wilderness; their walk with God through it all, and the 'looking forward' to the promised land. A whole generation has passed. Now Moses addresses this emerging generation – reminding them of their past, but also the anticipation of what's to come. Sadly, the generation that was delivered from bondage in Egypt would not enter the land of promise, mainly because of disobedience. But there was hope for the new generation. They were to be God's people for the future.

Sometimes we feel uneasy about emerging generations. They think differently from us; they act differently; they have ideas that are hard for us to swallow at times. The world that surrounds us looks so vastly different from the world ten or twenty years ago. We often feel we're gasping for air, not knowing where we even stand on various issues that are arising.

Just two years ago a British scientist, Robert Edwards, received the Nobel prize in medicine for developing the first test-tube baby, a technique called *in vitro fertilisation*. Now, Louise Brown is thirty-four years old, having a child of her own. Thirty years ago, however, we didn't know what to think. We had to really trust the Lord with what was happening all around us. Yet now, so many couples are using this widely accepted method to help them have children. God creates, and we leave it with him how this is done.

The emerging generation – with all their technological expertise, and their very different ways of doing things – need us, as we need them. Can we encourage them, challenge them, support them – as Moses did – for all that lies before them?

Thought

Why not make contact today with someone from the emerging generation, to have coffee and conversation with them. Tell them you'll pray for them and support them in their walk with God.

With You

The LORD your God has blessed you in all the work of your hands (v. 7).

The book of Deuteronomy was written for the people, for the community, for the 'church' of Israel. Yes, it speaks to issues concerning the law; but more than this, it is a gospel of redemption – in that God saved them from bondage and now has brought them to himself in a covenant relationship. He wants this new generation to feel secure in his love, and so encourages them by promising to them a land they can call their own.

Why is this book important, and considered to be inherently great in itself? Not just because it's a reminder of what happened before; but rather, what was lying ahead for the people. After forty years, something was now going to happen – and it was imminent. Also, we witness God breathing into his people a renewed vision of who they were in him. They had everything, for God was with them:

These forty years the LORD your God has been with you, and you have not lacked anything (v. 7).

Powerful words then; powerful words for today. To know that God has been there, and will continue to be there, always. His love is unmerited; but it is extravagant, and available to all who trust in him. Even though some of us have been through storms, through difficult times, through 'wanderings' like the Israelites, God is always present. We might not always acknowledge him; we might not always feel this presence; but he is always there.

How do we know for certain his direction for our life? In verse 2, God tells Moses the people have wandered far enough. God assures them of what's ahead, and of his continual presence by simply saying, 'Now turn north.' Specific guidance, direction and instruction – leading to the land of promise.

Today, let's listen intently to his voice, turning in the direction God has for us. He will lead on to wonderful destinations; and he'll be *with* us, every step of the way.

Social Justice

All your able-bodied men, armed for battle, must cross over ahead of your brother Israelites (v. 18).

No person's good is greater than the good of all. The *good* rests with the loyalty and service of each person. In other words, I am not truly safe until *all* are safe and secure. And if we extend this even further, I am not content until freedom and democracy are assured for all peoples. No individual nation is safe, until there is security and freedom for all. United together in a bond of love is the ideal; to be secure in Christ Jesus' eternal love for his people.

The area east of the Jordan was to go to Reuben, Gad and the half tribe of Manasseh. For its conquest, *all* the 'able-bodied' men were needed. The task ahead of them required full participation – by everyone. Together, they would do what God required, even if it directly didn't benefit them personally. They were to do it, because it would benefit another; and in the end, all would be safe and well.

We are part of individualistic societies and cultures. Yet we are all very much connected to one another. Traditionally, there has always been some kind of *invisible* line, dividing those who needed help from those who gave it. But things have changed somewhat because of social breakdown, and individual choices made – sometimes causing damage to both the individual and others; thus, proving once again the need of one another.

Because we're all connected, because we all have *heart* and have a great concern for each other, we need to make sure we all have the same common goal – to reach out, beyond ourselves, to make this world a better place in which to live. This can only be done through Christ, and his indwelling Spirit. It can only be done when our soul reaches out, to connect with another soul.

Prayer

God, may I look beyond my own sphere today, and pray for justice to be done throughout your world. Today, may you bring to all people your perfect strength, comfort and peace. Amen.

Peter – the Leader

'And I tell you that you are Peter, and on this rock I will build my church'
(v. 18).

Peter was bold, forthright, reactionary, impulsive, impetuous. But, above all, he was a born leader. He was the one who seemed to pull things together. A dominant figure; yet one who was needed in the group, no question. An extrovert. However, he was also acutely sensitive. He seemed to know his heart well.

What kind of characteristics do we see in Peter, the leader? He was *humble*. One time, the fishermen had been out all night but had caught nothing. Jesus stood at the Sea of Galilee and simply told them to let down their nets once more. Peter, the leader, didn't mention that he knew more about fishing than Jesus; nor did he protest about the request. Rather he simply obeyed, and their nets almost broke with all the fish caught.

When they approached shore, Peter ran to Jesus, throwing himself at his feet – telling Jesus to go away from him, for he was such a sinful man. Jesus responded to Peter by affirming him, and in fact commissioned him:

'Don't be afraid; from now on you will catch men' (Luke 5:10).

Peter was a man of *faith*. Jesus was walking on the water, coming toward the disciples in the boat. When Peter heard Jesus' command, 'Come', he quickly got out of the boat in faith and walked toward him. Well, you know the story. He looked down, became fearful, then started to sink. Jesus was right there to help him. Yet this experience made his faith even stronger.

Peter was also a man of *conviction*. When Jesus asked him: '*Who do you say I am?*' (*Matthew 16:15*), Peter responded: '*You are the Christ, the Son of the living God*' (*v. 16*).

Humility. Faith. Conviction. No, not perfect; but we also know of Peter's repentant heart. And so, today, may we be people with these same qualities – giving our very best for Christ.

Peter – My Moving Story

The third time he said to him, 'Simon son of John, do you love me?'
(v. 17).

You probably know more about me than you do of most of the others. You know some of my good traits (or so they tell me); but you also know of many of my terrible traits. I tended to react to things; I often spoke out before thinking; I was upfront about my opinions – and usually acted upon them right away.

What kind of personality type would you label me as having? You know all too well. It definitely gave me strength; but it also got me into trouble.

Of course, you also are fully aware of what happened at Jesus' trial. He'd predicted I'd deny him; but I honestly never thought I would. It's something I've had to live with ever since. I've also had to live with the consequences of my sin. But there *is* life after having messed up big-time – when we are truly repentant. God forgives, and he also forgets. It's us who still hold on to things.

It was early in the morning, following his glorious resurrection. Jesus was cooking us breakfast – can you imagine? He suddenly turned to me, asking me if I loved him. In fact, he asked me this same question three times. Maybe it was because I had denied knowing him three times. Maybe it was because he just wanted to be sure of my love for him, my commitment to him. I'll be honest; it hurt me at first – his questioning me like this. But I realised he was strengthening me through it all. He was making sure I was strong in my deep devotion to him; for the road ahead would not be easy for any of us. And he had chosen me to be the 'Rock', the leader of this new and powerful faith called Christianity. '*Feed my sheep*,' he had said (*v. 17*). The 'Rock' needed to be a firm foundation for the others, for Christ's sake.

And so I say to you fellow believers, fellow followers of Christ Jesus, be strong in your faith – no matter what you will face today, or tomorrow. Above all, I urge you to respond to Jesus by saying:

'Lord, you know that I love you' (v. 16).

Trusting

Trust in the LORD with all your heart and lean not on your own understanding (v. 5).

Worry. It's a plague, really. But we all have to deal with it, at some time or another. And some have to work on this much more than others. We can worry about a poor outcome, a poor ending to a certain problem, and make ourselves physically ill. Stress. More worry. It's all about the 'what if' aspect. It can consume us. It can affect us spiritually. We feel out of control. We don't know what to do with everything going on inside.

One day my youngest daughter Kirsten, when a young teenager, said to me: 'Worry is a sin.' I was really thrown by this statement, ready to dismiss her words. Then I suddenly thought, yes, she's probably right! It's a lack of trust in God. For don't we say he'll take care of *everything*? My Lord, my God, cares enough about me – my life, my family, my situations – and only wants the very best for me. What must I do, then, in response to this profound awareness?

In all your ways acknowledge him, and he will make your paths straight (v. 6).

In everything I do and say, I am to give witness to Christ. In my home, I am to put God first in all things. At work, I am to constantly be aware of others and to be God's instrument of peace and joy. Also in my 'play' time, when I'm relaxing and just seeking some form of entertainment, may all I see, read and do be God-honouring.

We must be a trusting people, especially when it comes to our relationship with God. For he knows beginning to end – and will always be with us.

Thought

Today, let us glorify his name by acknowledging our trust in him. And let us simply enjoy fellowshipping with him, by delighting in his presence!

It Is Well . . .

The LORD *turn his face toward you and give you peace (v. 26).*

> When peace like a river attendeth my way,
> When sorrows like sea billows roll,
> Whatever my lot, thou hast taught me to know
> It is well, it is well with my soul.
>
> *(SASB* 771)

This moving hymn, by the American lawyer Horatio G. Spafford, was written after he received news of his four daughters being drowned at sea, en route with their mother to Europe in 1873. Travelling to bring some kind of comfort to his grieving wife, while trying to keep together emotionally himself, Spafford came to the approximate place on the Atlantic where his daughters had drowned. It was there, on the boat, where he penned these words. He had no explanation for the horrific tragedy; he didn't know how they were going to get through this dark time in their lives. But he trusted in the Almighty:

> Though Satan should buffet, though trials should come,
> Let this blest assurance control,
> That Christ hath regarded my helpless estate,
> And hath shed his own blood for my soul.
>
> *(v. 2)*

How could he write words reflecting assurance and peace within after losing his four precious daughters? We can't even begin to imagine. All we do know is that, when trials and suffering come, God promises to be there with us – to help us get through, no matter how difficult the situation may be.

It is when we feel so alone, so abandoned, so helpless, that he comes to be with us – giving us a peace like we've never experienced before. It is then, and only then, that we can sing with the writer:

> It is well, it is well with my soul.

Generational Inheritance

Just make sure you stay alert. Keep close watch over yourselves. Don't forget anything of what you've seen. Don't let your heart wander off. Stay vigilant as long as you live. Teach what you've seen and heard to your children and grandchildren (v. 9, MSG).

Many of us have children, and some of us are also privileged to have grandchildren. Today's verse, uttered hundreds of years ago, reminds us to share our experiences of God with the next generation. We're to talk with them about the trials, the difficult times – and God's presence through it all. We're to share with them the blessings and the joys, all because of God's presence.

If some don't have children, we are to share these important life experiences with nieces, nephews, children of friends. After all, God has given to all of us certain wisdom and insight. The oral tradition for communication has somehow been lost. Yet how important it is – to be *vigilant*, as Scripture says, and keep it going; for wisdom and experience are rich and valuable and to be treasured.

Moses, as he was speaking to the Israelites, felt this was vital, if God's name was to be truly honoured. Two chapters later in this same book we find the same kind of instruction. Let us 'listen' to his words and take heart, as we try to think how we can pass on the 'testimony' of our lives to the next generation:

Write these commandments that I've given you today on your hearts. Get them inside of you and then get them inside your children. Talk about them wherever you are, sitting at home or walking in the street; talk about them from the time you get up in the morning to when you fall into bed at night (6:6, 7, MSG).

The next generation should see Christ shining through us. If this is true, we need to – we *must* – talk about this with them. Ah, we say, we still mess up; we're not perfect. Yet hasn't God done marvellous things in and through our lives worth sharing?

Yes; may the Lord help us *all* to pass on to younger generations what he has done in our lives. It will, indeed, be a blessing – for all!

Obedience

'Who can stand up against the Anakites?' (v. 2).

The command 'Hear, O Israel' is stated over and over again throughout the book of Deuteronomy. Moses was making a pointed appeal to the Israelites for *obedience* to God. He already reviewed the Ten Commandments with them, the moral and spiritual requirements for humanity. For he wanted the people to pass them on to succeeding generations. And through it all, he told them that complete obedience was essential, if they wanted to conquer their foes in God's strength.

Who, then, were the foes? The sons of Anak – the Anakites – were a definite threat to the Israelites. They were a race of giants, greatly feared, living in Canaan. In the book of Numbers, they are mentioned several times, as reported by the spies:

'We even saw the descendants of Anak there . . . We saw the Nephilim there (the descendants of Anak come from the Nephilim). We seemed like grasshoppers in our own eyes, and we looked the same to them' (13:28, 33).

For years these towering giants were a haunting symbol of the Israelites' fear – resulting in their unbelief in the power of God's presence with them. And so the question begs us: Who are the 'Anakites' we face? What keeps us from being obedient to God? Oh yes, we might be doing many things that are right. We might be obedient in certain things, and even in the eyes of others. But deep down, are there things God wants us to do that we're desperately trying to ignore – because of various circumstances?

Moses assured the Israelites that God specialised in dealing with 'Anakites'. God would go before them, and they *would* inherit the promised land. Are there things in our way, stumbling blocks, even 'people situations' that are hindering our spiritual progress? All God wants from us is our obedience. To trust him implicitly. For, when our hearts are filled with faith, there is no room left for fear. We are to trust and obey; for, really, there *is* no other way.

Pierced Ears

If your servant says to you, 'I do not want to leave you' . . . then take an awl and push it through his ear lobe . . . he will become your servant for life (vv. 16, 17).

Slavery was very common in the ancient Near East, and thus God's people were no different. The Israelites themselves had been slaves in Egypt; it had been a very difficult time for them. But the slavery spoken of here was quite different. Slaves were often purchased to be of help to the household; and usually, slaves were treated almost as part of the family. Yet, they were still slaves. They did not have complete freedom.

Slavery did not fit well with God's emphasis on the equality of all people. The prophet Isaiah, later in time, uses these words, quoted several hundred years even later by Jesus himself:

The Spirit of the Sovereign LORD is on me, because the LORD has anointed me to preach the good news to the poor. He has sent me to bind up the brokenhearted, to proclaim freedom for the captives (61:1).

Therefore, a new law is being established here in Deuteronomy. One could now purchase a slave, but to serve for six years only. In the seventh year the slave is to be released, set free. However, if the slave had been treated well, feeling part of the owner's family, he could ask to remain with his master – to be protected, to work for him, to feel secure, even to be both loved and accepted. As a perpetual sign of this new relationship, the master would pierce the servant's ear – proclaiming to all: 'This is my beloved servant; I am his beloved master.' The psalmist David picks up this very image:

'Sacrifice and offering you did not desire, but my ears you have pierced . . . I desire to do your will, O my God' (Psalm 40:6, 8).

Whether we have pierced ears or not, when we see them on others let it be a reminder that we are Christ's loving servants. May we give our ears, our life, to him afresh today.

Paul – from Darkness to Light

I thank Christ Jesus our Lord, who has given me strength, that he considered me faithful, appointing me to his service (v. 12).

Paul was a student of religion; a well-educated man; a Pharisee. He knew the law well, and was a well-respected Jew. He had come across various sects before – people who had far-fetched ideas and philosophies. He had even been well exposed to the Greek gods and their various legends. But they were all myths.

Now, here was a group claiming Jesus of Nazareth was the promised Messiah. Jesus, the son of a carpenter. Jesus, who looked and dressed like everyone else. Jesus, who grew up with brothers and sisters like the rest of humanity. This same Jesus who was now claiming to be God's Son. Absurd! An insult to all Jews. Paul felt this movement needed to be stopped – before things got out of hand. For people were even willing to give their lives for him.

He began to persecute believers. He stood and watched, as Stephen was stoned to death. Paul felt he was fully justified in stomping out this new group, this sect, in order to preserve the dignity and tradition of the Jewish faith. After all, they were the chosen people of God. Paul was a man of deep convictions. His hatred for these Christians was real. It seemed to consume him.

He was destined to go to Damascus, and we know the story well. The flash of light, the blindness, the complete turnaround of a strong and vibrant personality. From darkness to light. From death to life. A complete transformation of character. Truly, and literally, a Damascus-road experience. A vision of Jesus.

He needed to get away to the desert. To pray, to read Scripture, to fast, to commune with the Lord, to be humbled, to be fed, to be energised – all for the great mission that lay before him.

So today take time, from probably a very busy schedule, for some solitude; time to just *meditate* on Christ. He will refresh; and he will give you a new vision of his purpose for your life – equipping you to minister even more effectively, all for his sake.

Paul – My Humble Story

'And now what are you waiting for? Get up, be baptised and wash your sins away, calling on his name' (v. 16).

I was anything but humble. In fact, I used to hate that word – for it had nothing to do with leadership, or strength of character. Humility was for the weak in society; those who couldn't get their act together. Whereas I was a strong Jewish leader, one who people looked up to and admired. I had made it in this world. A man of substance. A man to be feared.

But that great flash of light, on the road to Damascus, changed everything. For the first time in my entire life I was deeply humbled. Yes, because I was physically blinded. But far more than this; I knew I needed to be stripped bare, humbled completely, before I could truly do anything good in my life for God.

It took time for the believers to trust me, and I don't blame them for this. I had been their main persecutor. I had been cruel and hateful, beyond belief. I had done major damage. But I kept praying for God's perfect timing; for I knew there was much to be done, and that God had a definite purpose for the rest of my life.

When I started my ministry, my various journeys into missionary territory, people admired me. My carnal nature ate this up – because in my former life I lived for this kind of praise and glory. I had to really fight this, and bring it before the Lord constantly. I was *nothing* without Christ. I could say this, verbally, to others because it sounded good. But I really had to believe it, and live it; otherwise, my ministry, my influence would all be in vain. Yes, I was a leader and had certain skills and gifts. But I realised they were all given to me by my Lord. Any results, any conversions, any transformation in people – it was all Christ's doing, not mine. I was merely a vessel; his humble instrument. *All* for Jesus!

And so, my dear brothers and sisters in Christ, I urge you to use the gifts and talents and skills God has given to you – only for him. Like me, pray for humility of spirit, daily. Then pause . . . look into the face of Jesus. Do you see him smiling upon you?

Taking Flight or Refuge?

How then can you say to me: 'Flee like a bird to your mountain'? (v. 1).

It is so easy to take flight, isn't it? When a problem arises, when people hurt us, when difficulty lies right in front of us – we want to escape, hide, run, even disappear. After all, who wants to deal with tough situations? We feel we're not strong enough emotionally, at least with this particular issue. It has maybe caught us off guard; it has thrown us, completely. We don't think it's fair at all; but also, we don't really want to talk about it, for it's private. We feel very frightened and alone.

David was a strong personality, a great leader, a man of God. The advice given to him, when facing a very difficult situation, was to 'flee like a bird'. He could have done this, quite easily. But what good would it have done? Yes, it might save him from facing the issue right at that moment. But it would soon catch up with him. And as it happened to David, it will happen to us.

What will we do when things come upon us? The key is to face things and to deal with them, with God's help. It's fully trusting in him, and abiding in him. How does David ultimately respond? It's his opening statement of this psalm:

In the LORD I take refuge.

God is our strength, our hiding place. And in that place he equips us, and helps us face all difficulties. He is there to hold us, and to comfort us. When?

When the foundations are being destroyed (v. 3).

God doesn't promise us that everything will be easy in life. Sometimes our 'foundations' are shaken – badly. This is when we need to take refuge in the one who made us. Our Father. And so, today, may he be your strength. Then, may you be a strength, a stronghold, for others – as God continues to live in and through you, day by day.

'Mid All the Traffic

The effect of righteousness will be quietness and confidence forever (v. 17).

The beautiful words of "Mid all the traffic' were written by William A. Dunkerley, using his pen name John Oxenham, in 1916. He wrote them from a small chapel, a place where there was 'an abode of peace'. Solitude. Quietness. Away from it all. Silence. It's quite different from what's out there in the world today. Road rage is prevalent in many cultures. The everyday noise of life; on the roads, in the streets, at work. Even people, yelling and screaming at each other – for no apparent reason.

It's not only the outside noise we have to deal with; it's all the noise in our head. Conflicting noises, telling us to do this and that. How can we turn it all off? How can we be quiet before the Lord?

> 'Mid all the traffic of the ways, Turmoils without, within,
> Make in my heart a quiet place, And come and dwell therein.
>
> *(SASB 615)*

What a beautiful thought! God, dwelling in my heart, in quietness. My heart – which is only for him.

I personally love this hymn because of its simplicity; yet also because of its deep implications relating to my time with God. Most of us long for a few moments, each day, just to experience his grace:

> A little place of mystic grace, Of self and sin swept bare,
> Where I may look into thy face, And talk with thee in prayer.
>
> *(v. 3)*

The hymn concludes with the following lines, which speak for themselves. For God can provide solitude and silence, a place for intimate communion with him. But we have to *want* this. He will never force it upon us. Do you want to be with him today?

> Come, occupy my silent place, And make thy dwelling there!
> More grace is wrought in quietness Than any is aware.
>
> *(v. 4)*

A Safe Place

Build roads to them and divide into three parts the land the LORD your God is giving you as an inheritance, so that anyone who kills a man may flee there (v. 3).

Refuge. Mercy. Security. A safe place. In the time of Moses, as the children of Israel were preparing to enter the promised land, there was an awareness – coming from the nomadic society of the day – concerning the whole idea of revenge. Yet God knew that if a death was unintentional, there needed to be places of refuge; cities set aside where people, who accidentally killed someone, could go and feel secure and protected. A safe place.

For the past four months we have shared together in these daily readings. As you have read these devotionals, I trust you have found your reading time to be a 'safe place' with the Lord. It sounds so simple, doesn't it? But we all need safe places. We all need to have that time alone with God – no matter where we may find ourselves.

We might be reading in the morning, together with our spouse or a good friend. We might read on our own, in the quietness of our home, or at the office. It's that safe place, where you and the Lord are together, in communion. It's an intimacy you share. A safe place where, for at least a few moments each day, the cares of the world vanish and can't snatch you away. A safe place, where you can trust God completely – with *everything*.

Personally, it's been a complete *joy* and deep honour for me to share with you in this way. I have been truly amazed by how God's Spirit has directed. And so, I wish to pray with you:

Prayer

My gracious Lord and Saviour, thank you for this readership. I ask your special blessing and anointing upon each and every one – for today, and all the tomorrows to come. May your peace be theirs, I pray. Amen.

Notes

1. C. S. Lewis, *Miracles*, Collins Fontana Books, UK, 1947.
2. Augustine of Hippo, *City of God*, Penguin Books, England, 1972.
3. Source: www.wycliffe.org
4. William Shakespeare, *Macbeth*, Act 5; Scene 5.
5. Bart Millard, *I Can Only Imagine*, © 2001 Simpleville Music, Inc.
6. Marcus Dods, *The Gospel of St. John, Vol. 11.* © Funk and Wagnalls, 1900.
7. Alfred Lord Tennyson, *In Memoriam A.H.H.*

Index

Subscribe . . .

Words of Life is published three times a year:
January–April, May–August and September–December

Four easy ways to subscribe
- By post – simply complete and return the subscription form below
- By phone – +44 (0) 1933 445 445
- By email – mail_order@sp-s.co.uk
- Or visit your local Christian bookshop

SUBSCRIPTION FORM

Name (Miss, Mrs, Ms, Mr)..

Address ....

....

.... Postcode ....

Tel. No. ....

Email* ....

Annual Subscription Rates
UK £12.50   *Non-UK* 12.50 + £3.50 P&P = £16.00
Please send me .... copy/copies of the next three issues of *Words of Life*
commencing with **May–August 2012**

Total: £ .... I enclose payment by cheque ☐
Please make cheques payable to *The Salvation Army*

Plese debit my Access/Mastercard/Visa/American Express/Switch card

Card No. ☐☐☐☐ ☐☐☐☐ ☐☐☐☐ ☐☐☐☐   Expiry date: ___/___

Security No. ☐☐☐   Issue number (Switch only) _____

Cardholder's signature: .... Date: ....

Please send this form and any cheques to: **The Mail Order Department, Salvationist Publishing and Supplies, 66–78 Denington Road, Denington Industrial Estate, Wellingborough, Northamptonshire NN8 2QH, UK**

☐ *We would like to keep in touch with you by placing you on our mailing list. If you would prefer not to receive correspondence from us, please tick this box. The Salvation Army does not sell or lease its mailing lists.